WHY WOULDN'T I?

PADDY FLANNERY

AS TOLD TO **EIBHLÍN WARD**

For my wife Mary and for my family, Martin, Patrick, Maria, Paul and Julie

Contents

Preface

"Paddy, how are you? Sorry I am late, looks like it was a great evening."

"It was, it was indeed, a grand evening alright."

I sensed there was something amiss. Paddy looked distracted, not really present in the moment.

"Do you know something though," he continued, "I was talking to a fella earlier and something he said brought me back. Nothing bad at all but it just got me thinking, made me think of school. He knows people I know, and I remembered the time the teacher gave me the shilling for working out a sum, did I ever tell you that one?"

"Sure, you did Paddy, an amazing story and why on earth are you thinking about it now, when you are hosting your company Christmas do?"

"God knows why, it just came into my mind, maybe I was thinking that life is strange and such a lot has happened, we've all come a long way."

"You have an incredible story," I mused. "I'd love to write it with you."

Paddy and Mary are salt of the earth people. I met Mary years previously at a football match with our children. We grew in friendship having so much in common. We spent many Sunday evenings sitting around their table, chatting about the work, chatting about life in Ireland, about opportunities in England. We came from Gaeltacht areas in Ireland and although geography and a few years separated us, circumstances and a fondness for chatting brought us together.

I had the privilege of listening to Paddy's stories and was delighted to work with him to put his memories on paper. This story is a fitting tribute to a great friend. It will also be a gift from him to his grandchildren and maybe also a gift for others to understand his remarkable journey.

The wisdom of the ancestors is a thread throughout this book. Paddy lives by the old sayings (seanfhocail or Irish proverb) that are quoted in this book. He is a very proud Joyce Country man and has set out to show how the land and the people that made him, never left him.

With gratitude,

Eibhlín Ward

Chapter 1
Cowboys and Indians

Myself, Tommy Joyce and Mairtín Sheain were down at the lake, our usual haunt after school. We were engaged in a wild, tumbling game that we called "American Boxing," a game that involved lunging, prodding, chasing and generally beating the hell out of one another with long brown sally rods we cut precisely for this purpose. We imagined that the rods, cut from the willow tree, were fine arrows. We used them to subdue our opponents and sometimes to sacrifice each other. Tommy would lie outstretched, arms flailing, begging for mercy, and either myself or Mairtín Sheain, as his brutal captors would be sure to offer no mercy. Ten years earlier, the film "The Quiet Man" had brought fame and fortune to the town of Cong, an eight-minute drive from Clonbur. Etta Vaughan from neighbouring Cornamona had been a stand in for Maureen O'Hara's character. Not much happened in Kilbride, we were proud of any vague connections to Hollywood. The film released in 1952 had brought tourists flocking to the area and had led to many tourist attractions being set up. The shop in the film had been turned into a pub, there were 'Quiet Man Tours' and souvenirs all set up for the tourists. This film showed the Irish in a way that the American audiences wanted to see. We didn't recognise the way the people were in the film at all. The dialect was not one which we knew, and only a smattering of Irish was used, everybody in the place seemed suspiciously handsome. It was in no way a reflection of the life we knew. All we, as young fellas, really took from the film plot was the boxing. Oh, how we loved the boxing! We had seen the scenes many times in the marquee erected across the lake as our makeshift cinema. My father used to row us across the lake with a couple of pennies in our pockets. We were delighted, thrilled at the prospect of spending them to sit on wooden benches in a draughty tent with a creaking projector whirring noisily as it struggled to bring great western films to life. We loved John Wayne in the westerns, but we didn't like him at all in The Quiet Man, he wasn't what we wanted at all. The only time he went up in our estimation was when his character Sean fought with a man called Will. We thought this was mighty altogether and acted out the brawl over and over again and turned it into our own game of American Boxing. We thought John Wayne was much better as a cowboy and we wished that instead of a soppy romantic film, John had made a western in Cong and brought some real-life Indians with him instead. In our childish play, we liked to imagine that this was in fact what had happened, and these Indians had arrived on the shores of the lake unknown to anybody. We spent many a summers evening stalking them like we had seen John do in his westerns. That was why we needed sally rods.

We crouched down on our bellies, and manoeuvred into position, we imagined wigwams and smoke signals above the lake. We moved, snake like among the rushes, with sally rods pointed, ready to take down the Indians that we had seen John Wayne do many times.

The only effect that this blockbuster film had on our lives was to fire our imaginations. Tommy, Mairtín and I would shriek with laughter as we lay clutching full stomachs among the sally, larch and beech that surrounded Lough Mask, shouting and making a fierce growling noise that would send the gulls soaring high into the brilliant blue skies. That was how we spent our days-larking about down by the shore, skimming stones across the vastness of water, not a care in the world. We would enter the lakeshore, clambering over the wall, across the stony ground to spend what seemed like endless sunny days out in my father's boat. Other days, we were to be found poaching spawning fish in the river that meandered languidly in the shadows of Cnoc a Choirín, munching on bread and cheese secreted from the house, washed down by a bottle of fresh raw milk, stolen straight from the cow.

I remember well the day when myself and my cousin Pádraig Mike Bán caught a great trout, we couldn't take it home of course. We had one eye open for the bailiff who was only too familiar with our devilment. We were always ready to hop on our bikes and make a dash for safety the minute we saw him. It was all part of the fun. In any case we couldn't take our fine catch home, or we would get a clip across the ear for poaching. The day we caught that trout stuck in my memory for another reason too, it was 22 November 1963, the day the president of

America John Francis Kennedy (JFK) died. When we eventually made our way home that day, an ominous silence greeted us. My aunt Molly and my mother Julia were huddled around the wireless. Imprinted on my brain for ever, was the shocked atmosphere and the gravity of the situation. At that time JFK and Jackie's images hung proudly in every home in the land alongside a picture of Pope John VIII, such was the esteem in which this proud son of Ireland was held.

"We could have brought the trout back with us Pádraig, no one would ever have noticed," I whispered as I gazed around the room at the bent figures intent on catching every word from the ten o'clock crackling broadcast.

Just five months previously, JFK had been warmly welcomed as the first US president to visit Ireland. He had strengthened ties between the Old Country and the United States. His wit, his empathy and historic understanding of the political situation in the fledgling Republic had provided hope for the future and now it was stolen away. The mood of the nation was reported by Wesley Boyd, a former Irish Times diplomatic correspondent:

"It was as if news had come of the sudden death of a son or a father, at first no one wanted to believe that it was true, but as the radio and television bulletins came in, hope gave way to sorrow. Laughter died and gossip ceased."

Our trout had no place in such a morose company. Days were spent walking the hills and glens, running through the abandoned tumbledown cottages that pockmarked the landscape, relics of famine times. Our families had eked out a living here for generations. This was our birth right, our home.

Kilbride was steeped in history and tradition. At school we heard stories about Captain Boycott's evictions when he came to work the land around Lough Mask for the landlord Lord Erne. We heard about the atrocities of the Black and Tans and the ambush at Tourmakeady on 3 May 1921 during the Irish War of Independence. We never heard it at school but from the old folk we heard whispers about the Maamtrasna murders. However, these things were in the past and held no interest for us. We looked to the future.

We knew these stories as we knew every flower; every tree that grew around the shore; as we knew how to catch a gleaming pike or silvery trout and cook them over an open fire for the dinner. We understood the rhythm of the land; how to tend the soil to produce an abundance of crops for harvesting in the Autumn. We only took what we needed; we recognised the natural way of things. We went to the bog to cut turf to keep our homes cosy during the long winters. It was then the mist would come into the valley and swallow up every whitewashed cottage until there was just a vast nothingness. For some, it was a bleak and unforgiving landscape, but for us it was home, and we were content.

I hated school. It wasn't just that I disliked school, I really hated it. It was an endurance, and for me, a constant crushing blow to my self-esteem. I was very shy, the third of the Flannerys that headed off to what I would later refer to ruefully as my university, the only place of learning available to me. Jimmy and John had trudged the same brow beaten track before me, getting a lift every morning in the teacher's black Morris Minor. Maybe that made my ordeal all the worse. The poor woman was doing us a good turn, helping our family as she would pass our house on her way back the road towards the schoolhouse. I remember my first day vividly. I trembled with fear, I felt so shy. I wasn't used to crowds and that is what I saw before me, a big crowd of unruly children in one big room. I remember taking my seat on the wooden bench beside another new boy. He didn't seem at all bothered by the situation in which he found himself, he was shoving and fooling about. I furtively glanced around the room and saw the peeling paint glistening with condensation on its journey down the grey damp walls. The poster of the 1916 signatories loomed above me although I had no notion at that time why the seven, foreboding, stern looking men should have pride of place on the wall and why one of them wouldn't even look straight at me. Perhaps he knew something that I didn't yet know about this place, where the windows were so high I couldn't even look out at the lake.

The one-roomed school nestled at the side of the lake was surrounded by what was to become my safe space, the school garden. I would often stand there looking out over the lake admiring the beauty of the shining reflections on a cool calm summer evening, as well as the slightly menacing afternoons when the wind whipped up the waves that came crashing to the shore. I could see the beauty in every view. I would look at the towering hills surrounding our valley and imagine myself escaping over them, far beyond and far away from the torture within those four stone walls. I remember playing with Kathleen Welsh and her sister Bridie. Their job was to try to teach me what they knew and give the teacher some time to try to work with the other pupils who constantly demanded her attention. The teacher had no option but to get the older girls to teach us. It must have been really difficult for her, day in day out having about forty of us sitting expectantly in front of her. What that poor woman saw before her were forty souls destined for export. This, along with the realisation that no matter what she taught us, it made no difference at all. She would never change our destiny or make any difference. It must have really been a frustrating position to be in. Every year, more and more people left our lovely area resulting in the decimation of the school roll. By the time I left school, only thirty-two children remained in that one roomed school. People were leaving the area in droves, getting out if they could. For despite the beauty of the place, at that time there was a sense of desperation, a fleetingness, knowing that this lifestyle couldn't sustain us. We were living in an isolated splendour of a bygone life.

Our native tongue was Gaelic, the Irish language. The Gaelic began to die in some areas after the Great Famine but not in

Kilbride. So many Gaelic speakers either died or emigrated and those that were left viewed Gaelic as the language of the poor and vulnerable. Pre-famine times, British rule had put pressure on the schools to ban Gaelic and teach through English. When the Irish Free State was formed in 1922, Gaelic became the national language of Ireland, and the State established the teaching of all Infants through Gaelic. In 1960 a choice was given to educators to only teach Gaelic orally in Infant classes if that better suited the needs of the community.[1] The result was a decline in the teaching of Gaelic in schools except in areas such as Kilbride where the majority of the population still spoke Gaelic. Of course, that didn't suit everyone. In our school, Gaelic had become the language of learning, of conversation and of business. There was a recognition that this Gaelic landscape was changing, some families were bilingual and to counteract the possibility of English creeping into everyday conversation in an area considered to be a Gaeltacht (Irish speaking area), there was a strict rule that we could only speak Gaelic in school. To speak English at all was not only frowned upon but was punishable by corporal punishment.

"Cur amach do lámha" was the command to hold out a hand for whipping if English was spoken.

---

[1] CRIL Commission on the restoration of the Irish language 1964 An Tuarascail Dheiridh

For me and my family, it was always Gaelic we spoke at home, so we rarely got beaten for the offence of speaking English. However this was not the case for every family. Mairtín Sonny's mother came from Crossmolina so spoke English to him. The poor fella was constantly being reported for speaking English when he was outside in the garden.

"A Mhaistreas, tá Máirtín amuigh sa gháirdín ag labhairt Béarla" was the constant report. Teacher, Martin is out in the garden speaking English.

For pupils from other English-speaking families such as the Duffy's from the shop in Finney, it must have been really difficult. There was real breaking-up of the language at that time.

Another English-speaking area was Ballintobber from where my grandmother hailed. It must have been hard for her in her already unsettled life when she got married and arrived in Gaelic-speaking Kilbride. It's hard to believe such differences existed between places only twenty miles apart. I suppose the reality is that lack of infrastructure led to an isolation and a uniqueness of pockets of community not known today. I never gave much thought to it really and by the time I was old enough to realise that my grandmother was not local, and my mother had learned Gaelic in school, they could both converse so fluently that to me they were native speakers like everyone else around.

It was not the language that was difficult for me. It was not the maths and counting that proved beyond comprehension; I remember fondly playing with things for counting, having counters of all different colours and really enjoying learning maths. My issues lay in the fact that I was very quiet and shy. Other lads were, as I thought, very cheeky and forward. In other words, they displayed a confidence that was completely foreign to me. They seemed so at ease, and I remember thinking I would love to have that confidence, exuberantly telling stories, laughing and giggling as they recounted their tales. I envied their natural chattiness but knew it wasn't a trait I would ever display. I didn't know it then but there was worse to come. I thought the only difference between myself, and the other lads was my crippling shyness. I didn't realise that I was not destined to learn like them. I was what was referred to in those days as "backward at learning," I was good at sums but could not learn how to read or write either in English or Gaelic.

I suppose today I would be termed dyslexic. Back then though, I was just referred to as the fella who couldn't read like everyone else. I really felt it. When I was nine or ten, realisation dawned. I knew others had an ability denied to me, they were better at reading and writing than me; I knew then that no matter how hard I tried it would never be any different. I was crippled with embarrassment.

The teacher couldn't understand me or meet my needs. In her eyes, I was stupid. It wasn't her fault- she didn't have time to deal with everyone and most certainly didn't have the necessary training needed to allow me to access learning in my own way. Having said that, she never hit me like I heard other teachers did in those days. She really wasn't too bad. Combined with crowd control and too many children stuck in one room, the teacher had a lot to contend with. As children, we were restless and heedless. The result was that the poor woman, who must have been tortured in that one room without help, without guidance, used to put the lads out in the garden setting flowers. Our school garden must have been the loveliest for miles around, such was the attention it received. She assigned us tasks such as digging and setting onions as well as tending plants. Most lads worked outside, and the girls continued to learn inside. I suppose the teacher thought she would make workers out of us because the expectation back then was that everyone went to America or Britain.

Britain was widely known, and constantly referred to by the teacher as, John Bull's Country. One year after leaving school most pupils emigrated. There simply was no work to sustain the population of the area. Farms were too small, and families had on average six children. There was nothing else to do but to emigrate and try to find work to survive.

As we got older, we learned to speak a bit of English; the result of having a lesson for half an hour each day. It is amazing really that it was not considered more important to speak English. It really wasn't, we conversed in Gaelic with our friends. There was a tension between keeping our language alive, keeping our identity intact and of having enough English to converse with others once we left the Parish. In the Gaelic speaking area, identity, culture and language were intertwined and manifested in the use of the Gaelic language.

Jimmy Mhaire was good at reporting children to the teacher and on the odd occasion I spoke any English at all, I got myself reported. Jimmy used to torment me. He was very clever, and he could read very well. He didn't hide his enthusiasm for belittling me and he was quite evidently delighted with himself as every day he would sit beside me and have his hand up for spelling. His demeanour betrayed his pleasure at observing my discomfort and his gloating, when he saw how much I struggled, was a bitter pill to swallow. One particular day, I could take it no more. He was almost jumping out of his seat with excitement, shaking his whole arm because he knew how to spell a word, I looked at him and I just couldn't help myself. I belted him. I knocked him clean off his seat and he went crashing down to the floor. I saw the look of astonishment on his face as he turned to gaze back up at me just before I thrust back my desk and headed out to my favourite spot among the onion sets. That evening, the teacher called into my mother for a chat and admitted to her that she totally understood my motivation for belting Jimmy, however much she couldn't condone what I had done. She also laughingly agreed that she was never so delighted to see Jimmy get his comeuppance, she was fed up with his gloating herself!

In those days, the most widely used behaviour management technique in every school was a good old insult and the teacher was extremely clever at delivering a killer phrase. She had really perfected this technique. She would say:

"The only thing you are good for is working down the sewers in John Bull's country."

She was also so proud and concerned for the safety of her car that every single day she would ask:

"Feach ar an gcarr agus ar rothaí an carr" (go and check my car and the wheels of the car) and the poor unfortunate child chosen to check the car would come back to state:

"Ta an carr agus rothai an carr ceart" (the car and the car's wheels are fine)

She was clearly delighted with her car owning situation but extremely worried anything would happen to it outside on the road when she was inside teaching.

I remember picturing in my mind what I had heard from people who had worked in the expertly built Victorian sewers, and then looking around the dilapidated, one roomed hovel that passed for a school and thinking to myself that working in the sewer sounded infinitely better than staying where I was!

As I have previously said, I was always good at maths. True, there were children a lot better at maths than me, but I knew that at least in maths, I had some chance of understanding, I could have a go. One fine day, the teacher asked a "big" question. I knew it was a big question because the room fell silent. I could feel the tension building. The usual suspects were stumped and that gave me added eagerness. I knew the answer. I waited in amazement and when I realised the magnitude of what was about to happen, I trembled and gingerly put up my hand. I remember clearly, the teacher looked at me in pity. I could sense she was undecided about asking me, probably trying to save me from self-inflicted mortification, but as nobody else had their hand up, she wearily relented and gave me a go.

"Bhuel, a Phadraig, an gceapann tú go bfhuil and freagra agat?" She asked. (Well, Paddy, do you think you know the answer?)

I hesitated, for I knew the sound of the jeering laughter that would follow if I got the wrong answer. I stood up, sweat poured down my brow. My heart thumped. This was my moment, and I offered her my answer. I got it right. The teacher stared in amazement; the children glanced over in disbelief. The big fella in the corner had got it right. There was a collective gasp, then indecision, followed by cries of celebration. For the first time ever, there was an air of collegiality; everyone was swept up in the excitement of the moment. There was no jeering. Children, in the way of children all over the world took the lead from the teacher and she was so deliriously happy that she gave me a shilling. The shilling was offered as a prize; it was offered out of the goodness of the teacher's heart. For me however, it meant something else; it was the unwitting consolation of the general view of Paddy Flannery. They were happy for my success that day and they didn't see my embarrassment or sense my awkwardness as conflicting feelings of joy and anger welled up within my very being. For in my own mind, I thought, "Why wouldn't I know that?"

Máirtín glanced over at me. He understood as he saw my expression, my sadness at how little was expected of me. He went out of his way to cheer me up, that was why we ended up down by the lake that day, playing cowboys and Indians. I spent the shilling in Duffy's shop. I bought sweets for us to devour. Mairtín was delighted that I had won a shilling and even more delighted to enjoy the bag of sweets. We made a great plan to escape going to school the next day. We knew that Paddy O'Mallaigh and Awnie would be down cutting slits to seed potatoes, so we decided to hide on the teacher behind the wall. We knew she would call for us for school but wouldn't see us. She would drive by, and we would make our grand escape. Unluckily for us, my mother saw the whole episode and we were given our marching orders. We had to walk down the road in the rain to go to school. Another day of torture loomed. Mairtin didn't mind too much but for me, there was a nagging feeling inside me that nobody really knew my worth. Nobody, except myself.

WHY WOULDN'T I?

Chapter 2
Kilbride

There was nowhere else on earth like Kilbride. We wanted for nothing- or so I believed. We enjoyed sunny days down at the lake, where the majestic hills cast a protective shroud over us as we played outside. My father's clinker boat painted blue and white, sat gently rocking on the lake ready to bring us to the fishing grounds and provide us with hours of endless fun out on Lough Mask.

Our Parish, nestling in the foothills of the Finney Mountains, overlooking Lough Mask, was a glorious place to live. Houses were hunkered down for protection against the elements and shone in whitewashed glory on the rare occasion that the sun glanced across our skies.

For most of us living in these low thatched cottages, we lived contented lives. We knew of the stately homes in England, where workers from Parishes like ours were employed. We knew of the railways being laid, tunnels being dug and buildings arising from war-torn Britain, where the workers would banter "as Gaeilge." We had heard stories all about workers in 'John Murphy's hole' in London, where if a man couldn't speak Gaelic he would be totally lost on the job. We knew that to emigrate was our destiny, this was wholly accepted, and we also knew the rhythm of life in Kilbride meant that we would go along to

Halloran's in Clonbur for the cardboard suitcase, stuff it with clothes from Jack Chape's market stall, and then cross the water. Suitcases were the best-selling items in the shop in those days.

We had heard stories of the rich folks in England, however we also knew of the dingy tenements packed with Irish families eking out a living in the cities of Britain. Families like our own, who had closed the doors on their thatched cottages, and swapped them for life in a tenement block, working in factories, on farms, in the homes of the rich, leaving the old way of life and taking on the new. We, along with many other families, gave thanks for the life provided by migrant fathers who toiled England's soil, built England's roads, dug England's tunnels and built England up from its war-torn devastation, to provide for us. Fathers, who sent packages home at Christmas to make up for their absence, as they took on more shifts to make a better life for us at home. We knew who we were and our place in the world. We never questioned it, didn't expect and were delighted when the world didn't throw us too much to deal with. Life in Kilbride was marvellous, we were happy and contented in our youth.

My father, Máirtín Flannery was a small, stocky man, whose kindly eyes were fading in a glaucomic fog from the early age of forty-five. He walked with a straight back despite having spent many years bending down to pull beet. His kind and gentle manner belied a steely determination only ever observed on very rare occasions by those who crossed him. I am known to be like my father in temperament. He had a certain shrewdness about him that I am said to have inherited. Máirtín was an uneducated man, yet a man whose deep insight into human nature ensured that he understood exactly what he needed to do to succeed. He always maintained that the education received was superior when English rule was still in place. Ireland after the civil war was disorganised as it emerged from colonisation. It was a new State where leaders had to take on a totally different role and establish a constitution. My grandparents' stylised penmanship and ability to recite poetry and facts from their school days were skills not taught to my father Máirtín.

Our enjoyment of such an idyllic existence can also be attributed to my grandfather, Daidí Mór Flannery. He used to tell us about the land commission offer when families from poor holdings like ours were offered the chance to move to richer land, mostly in the East of Ireland. We heard tales of an April day in 1940 when two big buses brought seventeen families from Kilbride, Cornamona, Finney and Clonbur to the new places. My mother's brother moved to Westmeath but like Daidí Mór, my mother didn't want to go. Her uncertain start in life made her wary of being uprooted and she longed for security. I was too young to realise the full extent of it, although I heard my father talk. The small farms that families gave up were divided among other farmers, giving more to those who stayed. That meant that they had better opportunities for successful farming.

While it may have improved things for the crowd who moved East or to the Midlands, the problem was that it was harder on those who stayed behind. Those who left were in a strange place far from home where people had different habits, and those who stayed, well, they were lonely. For some of these split-up families, the result of the move was that they suffered a crippling loss that lasted for the rest of their lives and in many ways affected not only themselves but the future generations.

In 1956, The Flannery family only had eight acres of land. It wasn't the best land; it was rough. On paper, the whole relocation process looked favourable to my father. My uncle, Matty Joyce was granted forty acres of land in Meath in 1965. He decided to take the land commission offer and the bit of land that he left was given to us. Some people didn't have to go so far. For example, my neighbour Tommy O'Mallaigh only went to Hollymount, Toher, just up near Ballinrobe. If it wasn't for the hardship of leaving family land and leaving neighbours and extended family, it was a win-win situation. My father decided he wanted to go too when he was offered a place of forty acres in Dunshaughlin. He knew if he took up this offer, he would get plenty of work and stay in Ireland. My mother and my grandfather had other ideas; however, we had just had a new house built. Even though our farm was small, we were managing with my father's wages being sent from England. My father listened to the concerns of his father and sympathised greatly with my mother's viewpoint and eventually refused the opportunity. He turned down a lot when he refused that offer.

Much to his credit, it was never spoken of as a lost opportunity, I never once heard him recount what could have been. When he decided to stay in Kilbride, he had to forgo his chance to work in Ireland, stay with his family and perhaps have his children remain on Irish soil. He turned down modern conveniences, for even though we had built a new house in Kilbride, we didn't have an inside toilet in the new building and the electrification of rural Ireland was a long way off. I don't feel in any way that he was sad about his choice. He was a pragmatic man whose resilience and sense of self was deep rooted in his community. He was also a shrewd man who understood that inheritance was much more than wealth. By uprooting his family from Kilbride, he would be taking his family from the land and from the community. A community in the true sense, where each person depends on and helps the people around them. He understood communities such as ours. The community looked after its own. So it was, combined with my mother's reluctance to leave and Daidi Mór's willingness to contribute to family life, the decision was made. We were staying.

Without electricity or running water, life was very basic. The washing of the blankets every year was done on the lake where my mother used to go and heat water in big pots down by the shore on fires made from collected twigs strewn around the shoreline. The blanket washing was a popular event and involved all of us children jumping recklessly on blanket bundles before they were rinsed out on the lake and put on the foreshore to dry. Water from the lake was very important to us. We used it for making tea, for cooking, and for bathing in the tin bath on a Saturday night in front of the fire. This was the reality. I wonder how my father must sometimes have thought afterwards. Did he imagine a lifestyle for his family that was more modern? For him, staying in Kilbride would ensure he was tied to a migrant life, but if he ever thought these things, I never knew. He was a happy man who seemed to enjoy this lifestyle.

As my father spent most winters in England, Daidí Mór was the man about the house. We all helped around the farm as much as we could and even though I was a shy child, I used to get myself in a fair bit of bother on any occasion that brought about a change in our daily routine.

First Holy Communion time was a great occasion in our Parish. This was the day, in accordance with Catholic tradition, that all seven-year-old children received a sacrament of the Body of Christ for the first time. It involved all sorts of religious instruction, and it also meant that we got new clothes. Our mother was great at patching and sewing but, on special occasions like First Holy Communion, she travelled into Clonbur, to Jack Chape's market stall. She wanted to make sure we had the best clothes possible. Not only did we have to know all of our catechism off by heart, but we also had to look the part. So, mother saved up to buy new trousers and a crisp white shirt for the photograph. We were like kings and queens going from house to house to show off our clothes. We were delighted to be praised and told how holy we looked after our Holy Communion. Of course, for us the most important event was the collection. In every house the woman of the house would welcome us in, turn us around to look over the mighty spectacle we presented in our fancy clothes. Most times all the man of the house did was nod and ruffle our hair. Having stood awkwardly for several minutes, the woman of the house would make a show of secretly passing a couple of shillings to us with a wink and a shush, indicating that nobody should know about the little arrangement. As First Communicants, we were supposed to try to refuse the offering, but the reality was that we had already imagined it spent at the next fair day in Clonbur. We were all looking forward to going into school on Monday to compare how much each of us had made. Before the children of the Parish received the sacrament of Holy Communion, the sacrament of Reconciliation or Confession was to be made. This is a sacrament that requires immense soul searching to ensure that every sin is recounted in the confessional box so the priest can intercede to ask God for His Forgiveness. On the appointed day, I had considered all of my misdemeanours and headed off to the church with two equally repentant friends, Tommy Mairtín Sheáin and Johnny Welsh. It was a hard thing to think of the sins I had committed. Luckily, we were given fine examples of sins from the teacher, who used to ask us to think of times we had done something wrong such as telling lies, stealing, beating each other up and not saying our prayers. Her eyes glistened with amusement as she relished in reminding us of every possible combination of sin. I wondered did she have to tell the priest each time she threw the collection box for the

African babies at us or when she fired the glántór at Pádraig when he didn't know his tables. I thought about times I ran from the bailiff with my friends, the time when I cut my sister Mary's hair and then smashed an egg all over her head. I thought of the time I belted Jimmy Mhaire Theague. I had a lot of sins to consider. I tried with great difficulty to look as sorry as I could, full of repentance as I approached the church. On entering the hallowed building, I gazed up at the gigantic rose window with its collection of saints engraved in blue glass, names that seemed to judge my every move. I knew the names of these saints from the litany said after Mass and imagined Saint Enda, Saint Colmon, Saint Colmcille, Saint Ita and all their saintly acquaintances looking down on me with disapproval as I confessed what I had done to my little sister Mary. I don't know if it was sheer terror and imagined hellfire that caused it, but myself, Tommy and Johnny were outside the box, giggling and laughing with nervousness. We were clearly not behaving and following the strict rules regarding confession, where time must be spent on reflection and prayer. We obviously made enough noise to bring us to the attention of Fr. Canning who was inside in the confessional box. He heard us laughing and being generally disrespectful. Out he rushed, cutting a fearful figure in his dark robes and with a roar that rattled the stations of the cross hanging on the walls, he belted each of us across the head. I'll never forget the horror of the great wooden door opening and the priest, red-faced, eyes bulging out of his head with his huge, gnarled hand swinging and walloping us. We had to leave. We ran off beneath the statue of the Blessed Virgin, and in our imagination, we could see her eyes sorrowfully following us as we fled in terror. We were petrified and vowed not to say a word to anyone, such was the shame of it all. I don't know how we thought we could get away with it in such a small place after causing the priest to react like that. However, we lay low, three fugitives hiding out in the mountains around the lake. Everything was great until Monday morning when that torturer Jimmy began his own litany and told the teacher. I was sitting alone, not really listening and as usual doing everything I could to make sure I wasn't brought to the teacher's attention when I became aware of the buzz of excitement in the air and the menacing looks being hurled in my direction.

"Thainig an sagart amach..." (the priest came out...)

Jimmy Mháire Theague was flushed with excitement and in full flow, bringing such a story to his totally delighted audience. A whole hour he took, embellishing all the way as the teacher asked for every little detail. She wanted the whole story and seemed terribly interested in such a minor misdemeanour, probably imagining the priest, her boss, losing his temper with some local ruffians. I will never forget the feeling of foreboding that came over me as I listened, only half recognising the story myself, such was the exaggeration of the whole sorry tale by Jimmy. Being hit by a priest, a man of the cloth, was considered very bad luck. It was well known that other people who had been hit by such a holy man never did well. My mother was summoned to the school and once told of this terrible tale wanted to go to beg for forgiveness on my behalf and for the priest's blessing, in case I was in for a life of misfortune. Somehow, she had cause to reflect overnight, she saw sense and never did go to the priest. She must have decided to take her chances!

On another occasion, after a night telling ghost stories by the fire and listening to Máire Daithí swear she knew when death was approaching (because she had foresight, or a gift), I had a wicked idea. Máire maintained she saw ghostly lights out on the lake when somebody was about to die. She held the whole room spellbound as she spoke, and she was intent on portraying a spooky ghostly atmosphere where she herself would be regarded as a mystic. She droned on, caught up in her fantasy while her audience, not believing a word she said, were caught up in the story she told. I winked at my friend and shared my unholy plan; it was too good an opportunity for us to pass up on. The very next evening, we rowed across to the far side of the lake with a home-made raft, a bucket full of rushes and a paraffin lamp. Once across, we waited patiently until night descended. The lake was flat, without a ripple, and there were a few clouds in the sky to cover us, the fearless adventurers. We lit the paraffin lamp, placed it on a home-made raft and pushed it out into the inky darkness. Deed accomplished; we rowed swiftly back around the lake to wait for the light to be spotted. We were rewarded with a keening (crying) wail that could be heard up and down the valley as the poor woman spotted the light moving stealthily in her direction. Nobody ever reported us for scaring the poor woman so much even though there were a few knowing smiles the next day as the tale was recounted.

Prior to the new house being built, we lived in a small two room thatched cottage. It had seen better days, cosy though it was. My grandmother had passed away long before I was born, so I slept in the bed beside Dáidí Mór, where I felt comfortable and safe protected by this big man. At dinnertime, food was cooked on a huge open fire and consisted of hairy bacon and cabbage and our home-grown potatoes served in a ciseán (basket) made of reeds. The meal on the table was washed down with milk from our own cows. Sometimes we had pike or trout from the lake, caught when we put down our little clinker boat built by Coynan Mhuileann. We usually killed a goat and a pig every year; it was a very healthy diet. Without electricity, the pig had to be salted to keep it edible while the goat had to be eaten straight away.

Long summer days were spent in the bog where we cut turf to warm our homes. The hard-working donkeys carried creels of turf in caravan style. Usually there were eight donkeys trotting along the two-mile journey carrying the turf home. My mother used to bring back tea and food to everyone working on the bog. I don't know why, but the hunger pangs that hit on the bog hit early and lasted a long time. Everyone worked in the bog. The women used to foot the turf, which involved drying out each sod by standing it up on its end, balancing it against three similar stacked sods and finishing each little stack off with a sod balanced on the top. The men cut the turf with a sleán or turf spade after having paired the top sod off. The children helped make stacks. It was back breaking work. In later years we had tractors, but my most vivid memory is getting up at five and working till sunset at ten o'clock.

When we finished working in the bog and all the turf was neatly piled in stacks against the houses, our next task was to work with the hay. We worked hard. No wonder we were fit to work when we emigrated to England. We didn't feel poor. A lot of people had sheep and more land than we had. My father working in England meant that we might have had more cash, but everyone had plenty of food. As children, from March until September we were kept busy but after that there was no work to do. It was then we would make dens in the hedgerows, make a swing between the trees, play football in front of the house, skim stones on the lake and play "kick the can", knocking cans off the old stone wall.

Each year, at Christmas time, tinsel adorned every mantle in the Parish, sprigs of holly crowned every mirror and picture and looked magnificent against the distempered walls. The candles in each window on Christmas Eve lit the way for the Holy Family as we knelt to pray. We weren't great at the prayers in our house, not like some others in the Parish. We were too unruly and usually too excited for the icing on the cake and the jelly and custard that would come our way on Christmas Day. A little stocking would be left for each of us, full of sweets and maybe a little gun. I remember one Christmas, my sister Mary got a rocking duck and got so excited she pulled it too hard and broke it. She was devastated as it was her only present. My mother used to buy books and comics and did her best to cajole Mary with those. My mother really encouraged all of us who could to read. We loved to see what my father would send us in his Christmas parcel, and we imagined him out shopping for each of us in the brightly lit and glistening streets of London. Looking at that situation now, it seems heart-breaking that this hardworking man from 'Joyce Country' was denied family time at Christmas. I can only imagine him enjoying the thought of his family's delight back at home on Christmas morning, but that was the way it was. There was no time for sentimentality in our world as we clambered to the oil cloth covered table laden for Christmas dinner and jostled to sit on the handmade chairs whittled out by Coynan Mhuileann, Clonbur's master carpenter. Those not quick enough to the table would grab a seat on the bac, two little stone seats on the hearth.

To build the house my mother had saved £800. It was a new four-roomed house with a slate roof. To us it was massive, built by Tom Higgins from across the lake who was a great handyman and builder. I remember sometimes being cold in the new house, so my grandfather would call the dog to lie on me to keep to me warm in bed, where the flour bag sheets, expertly handcrafted by my mother, were wrapped tightly around me.

My mother Julia was a Joyce, whose father hailed from Coill Mór just back the road. Her mother was a widow from Ballintober whose husband, Jennings, had unfortunately drowned. She re-married and the Jennings children went to live with relatives. It wasn't uncommon in those days for children to be given to relatives when times were tough. Unfortunately, my grandmother then died very young of multiple sclerosis, so my mother and her sister were themselves fostered by relatives. In times when nobody had anything, this was a gallant thing to do, even though the families who took the children were not too well off themselves. This was certainly the case for my mother, whose kind relative Sonny Phaidí took her in. Because they lived a distance from the school, she used to walk five or six miles every day. The nuns had to dry her clothes over the fire after she arrived from her long trek. This made my mother a very resourceful woman whose determination and strength of character would see her have lots of successes in her life.

We were helped on occasion by those who had gone to England or America. There was excitement when we would receive some clothes sent from my father's brother, Cóilín, from Wigan. We felt like princes and princesses in these clothes as we argued over who would get what. As my mother was so careful with money, she only needed to buy flour, tea and sugar from Duffy's shop in Finney. Everything else was home grown. We wanted for nothing, although I do remember being mad jealous of Michael Eamonn who brought currant bread and biscuits to school. That family didn't stay too long in our Parish and moved on very quickly to Wicklow where perhaps currant bread was the norm.

In 1956, life was good. Like every family in the Parish, we had lots of relatives in the United States, and we called them Yanks. The Yanks were due home, and this was big excitement, so to celebrate we had a party in the new house. The dust was rising from the floor, that's how I remember it. That and the return of the Yank, Eibhlín O'Mallaigh. It was a grand occasion, the return to Kilbride of the wonderful Miss O'Mallaigh.

Eibhlín's brother Tommy was like most of the O'Mallaigh's, an accomplished musician. He played the accordion as sweetly as the dawn chorus and played tunes as lively as fish jumping in Lough Mask. The table bowed, laden as it was with porter brought to the gathering. People were ruddy-faced and glistening as they started doing cruiscíní, a wild type of dancing that mimicked the rise and fall of the mountains and that was as old as the lake itself. The wildness of the dance surged like the powerful waves that sprang out of nowhere on Lough Mask and then retreated like the gentle lapping on the rocky shores.

That night, everyone was in great form, ready for the gathering, to hear the latest news, to drink the finest porter, to listen to the sweetest tunes and to dance. It always struck me as remarkable how these burly farmers who toiled the rugged lands around the lake could be so light of foot and at one with the airs and reels, dancing seán nós to the tunes handed down from generation to generation. The new house was built, and it was a big deal. Everyone wanted to celebrate. The music was louder than I could ever remember, the accordions vied for attention as the raucous shouts and belly shaking laughter drowned out the tapping of many feet dancing the Siege of Ennis and the Walls of Limerick. Everyone gazed admiringly at the Yank, who seemed to shimmer like the lights of the dazzling city she had left behind. Everyone wanted to touch her, to be part of her story that night. They admired her as much as they admired the roughly plastered walls, eyes searching as they took in the dimensions of the new bedrooms standing proudly off the kitchen. I remember well the blue oil cloth covering the roughly made table and chairs in the centre of that fine room. It felt like a minor victory to stay and build a new house at home. That night nobody was in any doubt that Kilbride was the best place on earth. Usually there was lots of talk from the older people who were feeling a bit demoralised because the young were leaving. They considered that all our lovely valley was fit for was sheep and for sending the young ones away. Even at six years of age, watching the glistening Eibhlín O'Mallaigh, I wasn't so sure that the States or even England could be all that bad. We lived in the shadow of emigration, that's for sure.

Another childhood memory I have is visiting hospital as a child to have my squint straightened. I received a beautiful toy bus for my bravery. I was about six years old at the time and I have a strong memory of going with my mother on the crossbar of her bike to Ballinrobe, where we caught the bus to Castlebar.

My operation was to take place up in Dublin and of course nobody could leave the farm to accompany me and stay the six weeks it needed for me to get better. So, difficult as it is to believe, as a six-year-old it was arranged for me to go on my own. When we got to Castlebar, I had an overnight stay in the County Home, where lots of people stayed if they were infirm or had nobody to look after them. I remember it clearly, that large imposing stone building, being in a ward with lots of elderly women and feeling scared as I said goodbye to my mother who returned home to Kilbride. She had left me in the care of Tom Johnny, who was staying there because he lost an eye, and a fella called Coirín both originally from our Parish at home. The County Home was initially the workhouse for the area and despite being transformed to rest home status, it failed miserably to shake off the history of the place. It was huge, dark and dismal and, for me as a six-year-old Irish speaking child in an English-speaking world, utterly terrifying. Somehow, I managed to rock myself to sleep that night and wake the next morning for my long and arduous journey to Dublin.

Dublin was fascinating. I had never seen so many buildings, so many people and so much traffic but I have no memory of much else except humiliation. An incident occurred when I got out of the car. I was desperate to get the toilet and managed to make myself understood to the nurse by grabbing my crotch and dancing around until she pointed to a door and barked an order in a foreign tongue. I remember running into the toilet and peering around, the first thing I saw was a white bowl with what

I now know to be taps and then another white bowl-like object only larger next to it on the floor. It gleamed so brightly that I thought this couldn't possibly be to pee in, so I did what I thought was the best thing to do, I peed on the floor beside the large white object. When the nurse came in to find me, the look of disgust on her face, before the palm of her hand came crashing down to meet my cheek, is something I will never forget. She yelled something at me in English and literally threw me on the bed. It was clear that I had done something awful. It had something to do with the white bowl-shaped object that I realised, after some time, must be the toilet. I was totally taken aback to think that people actually peed in such a shiny, white glistening bowl with silver handles that washed the pee away. I had never seen such a thing in my life, not even in the County Home in Castlebar. Dublin, I thought to myself was an amazing place without doubt.

I was put into a ward with elderly men and noticed that the poor old devil in the bed beside me couldn't see a thing; he was totally blind. He also had a stash of chocolate biscuits in his locker; most of the men had. They had visitors who would bring them in bottles of lemonade, chocolate biscuits, grapes, and sweets. I had no visitors. I watched carefully and bided my time. Because of the vivid memories I had of the wallop from the nurse, and also because I understood nothing of what anyone was saying around me, I made myself as small as possible. I tried my best to remain unnoticed amidst the hustle and bustle of the busy ward. I sobbed silently to myself at night, not knowing how long I was going stay in hospital. I had no idea when I would see my family again, or no idea what was going to happen and felt terribly lonely. After a few nights, the thought came to me, I was desperate to taste the chocolate biscuits in the old man's locker. He had been kind enough earlier in the week to let me have one, so I knew exactly where he had them. I am ashamed to say, despite all the catechism I had learned from the priest, I waited for the opportunity to pounce. I knew I had to make sure there were no visitors, no nurses or doctors as I snuck stealthily out of my bed towards the old man's locker. I opened it as quietly as I could and carefully put my hand in. I could see the prize, the brown shiny paper with the top all screwed together to keep the biscuits fresh. I couldn't be sure if the old man was awake or not, but it didn't matter I reasoned to myself, he couldn't see me anyway. The biscuits were within my grasp. I lifted them out with the ease of a boy who had spent many evenings reeling in pike from Lough Mask. Up, up I lifted the packet and without rustling, released it from the dark depths of the locker, then crash! I felt, rather than saw, the stick hit me on the head, it laid me out flat on the floor followed by the old man screeching "you thieving little brat, clear out of my locker and leave the biscuits alone!"

I scarpered back to my own bed, pulled the sheets over my head and with my heart beating wildly, waited for the inevitable telling off or worse. Nothing happened. I can only conclude that the nurses must have felt sorry for me.

I left the hospital six weeks later accompanied by a Traveller boy on the journey back to the County Home in Castlebar. I was well used to Travellers as they were welcomed into my home every year on their way to sell their wares at the fair in Clonbur. Once again, we met the old women in the wards who were too infirm to look after themselves and once again, we stayed overnight. I liked the Traveller boy and was delighted to have the company. I could speak a bit of English after spending six weeks in the hospital in Dublin, so we made ourselves understood to each other in the way children do. The next day a taxi came for us to take us home, I was dropped off first and off went the taxi, with the Traveller boy who, sadly, I never met again. I used to look out for him every year when the caravans would pull into the field up the road and the women would go from house to house to sell their tins. The brightly coloured caravans were beautiful and when they rested their horses in our field, I used to go up to see if I could find him, but I never did.

There was a great welcome for me when I returned home. My family had missed me as much as I missed them. The operation was not very successful as I still had a squint. But, one thing I did have that was new and made everyone howl with laughter, was the ability to speak some English with a strong Dublin accent. So, there I was, entertaining everybody with the phrase, "I was up in Dublin," spoken like a true Jackeen, still squinting, but safe at home after a lone adventure which was, for a six-year-old, quite astonishing.

PADDY FLANNERY

Chapter 3
Stocach (Young Man)

At the age of thirteen my schooldays were over, and I was glad. My chances of success had been blighted so much by my inability to learn to read, that nobody had any expectation of me to go to the secondary school. My days in the small school had been spent gardening, even today the ruin is surrounded by a mass of montbretia flowers that I like to fancy I had a hand in settling into the worn soils of Mayo. The little school is in ruins but has the remains of a once glorious garden, thanks to me and a few others.

My mother was very interested in education. She knew its value and we were encouraged to read; books were bought at every opportunity, however my reluctance to read meant that she realised that she couldn't push too far. She wasn't too worried about me at all as she knew that boys could succeed by working hard. It was just as well they had faith in me to make something of myself because when I left school I still couldn't read or write, unlike my brother Jimmy, who was very clever, and won a scholarship. I remember my parents being so proud of him, they could see the possibilities in store for anyone who had a secondary education and they had saved enough money to buy the uniform for him to attend St. Jarlath's.

As the men in the area were mostly away working, the women were left to rear the children and keep the home fires burning. My father returned every year in February and told us grand stories about the towns he had visited and the places he had been. I used to listen in awe, repeating the strange sounding English names over and over again. We heard Peterborough as Peter Burra and Leeds as Leee-ds. Those sounds that didn't trip easily off our Gaelic-speaking tongues. For some reason, these names made me think of grand places full of splendour, and excitement as we imagined a great life where people wanted for nothing. As children we delighted in speaking to each other in strangled English tones, "And how do you do?" We would screech at each other in laughter, before replying, "I'm terribly well and you?" We would dart around the little house pretending to be English and not really having a clue what 'to be English' really meant.

Not every man from our Parish went to England as they didn't all have to; it may have been that their farms were better able to keep the families. Father worked with a lot of people from Kerry, Connemara and Donegal; seasonal workers who would go over to harvest beet in the vast rolling farms of England. The farmers would pay the workers' passage over and in return they would pick beet all day and live-in farm accommodation. It was a backbreaking hard existence, but the camaraderie got them through it, as everyone was in the same boat. The accommodation was divided one for the men and one for the women. There was a communal cooking area where the workers would gather after their days toil. Leisure was a scarce pleasure, sometimes they travelled into the nearest town for a few pints at the weekend or occasionally the younger ones would enjoy the local dances. It was a poor life, a hard life, but a life enjoyed by many without doubt. For some, the indignity of the lifestyle was a scar on the memory that they did their best to forget. Others didn't mind it at all.

I always remember that my father would get tax back when he came home, he was so proud of this as it declared that he was an honest man doing an honest day's work. Everything was above board and done properly. This would have a big impact on me in later years as I remembered the importance to all of us of my father getting his tax back.

My father was a gentle man whose presence at home meant that I could have a break from some of my responsibilities if not all. I noticed how he loved to sing Peigí Leitir Mór every morning as he rose early to get the fire ready for us before we went to school. He seemed to love the task of setting the breakfast table for us as we would clamber out of our beds. I saw how these small everyday actions brought a smile to his weary, kind and gentle face but in those days, I never thought about how much he must have missed the normality of family life as he worked with all the other Irish migrants on the beet farms of England. He was such a cheery character who never grumbled at all about his life, he never questioned it, just got on with it as did many more of his generation.

Now, I often wonder how it really was for him, coming home to his family who were growing up, setting potatoes he wouldn't harvest and living a sort of twilight existence between two worlds. He set the potatoes but was never there to dig them; he'd be long gone before that. As a child I was used to this and really looked forward to him arriving back home. That was the way, when he was home, he would get a bit of stamp money from England. It was a fine life for us and indeed for my father too. He lived his life with a stoic acceptance, like many more hardworking men of Mayo.

One of my friends, Tommy, loved working with my father and still talks about it to this day. He recalls better than I do, the hours spent on the farm saving hay that he had cut for them and the fun we had with Marcus Pat Mór. Marcus was a lovely fella who had a reputation for being the best pig killer in the Parish. He could do the job efficiently and humanely and so was in great demand. Tommy was great friends with him and would bring him along when we were saving the hay. As good as Marcus was at killing pigs, his expertise didn't extend to the saving of hay. But the promise of a drop of the black stuff at the end of a day's work was enough to get him to come along. The best place we had for him was at the top of the stack where he'd gather the hay together. Trouble was, as the stack grew higher, so did the distance between Marcus and the porter below. The fun at Marcus' expense would begin then, as he would be too high to jump down to get the much longed for porter and we'd tease the life out of him stuck at the top of the stack looking down at us guzzling stout. Looking back at it now, Marcus knew exactly what he was doing. He had an easy shift for the price of a drop, and he accompanied us every time, so he enjoyed the craic as much as we did. It was such innocent fun, and we made the most of it, almost as if we knew we were on borrowed time; our time to go was on the horizon.

Eventually over in England, my father got a better job with McAlpine and left the beet farms. This work was tough, but my father wanted to better himself so he could help my brothers Jimmy and John find work when they both went to England. Their departure brought about a big change in our house. It was the beginning of the erosion, stealth like, it crept in, expected, anticipated and unwelcome. That was one thing we could pay homage to the hills of Mayo for, men knew how to work. My father now had two sons to work alongside, with sub-contractors on the rail and it meant that they couldn't come home so often. I was now the man of the house aged fourteen.

I'm not sure whether my mother was hopeful that one day my literacy skills would suddenly emerge and make her son an academic learner. Whatever the reason, it was my misfortune to have to stay on in primary school. The local school I attended not only didn't cater for somebody with my dyslexic traits, but it also didn't cater for having a thirteen-year-old learning with all the younger children of the Parish. It never ever got any easier for me and so it was with sheer delight I finished school in January 1964. I still remember the feeling of happiness as I walked out of that school on my last day. I knew for certain that what I had gone through at school was not right. I had been subjected to years of torment, suffered humiliation as one by one, my classmates mastered literacy. I wouldn't say I felt sorry for myself at all, I really didn't, but I did feel an overwhelming sense of a job unfinished. It is a credit to my parents and my upbringing that my self-belief remained intact, and I promised myself then that I would never feel like that ever again in my life. I cast a backward glance and admired the school garden I had created as I left the tiny little schoolhouse. Who knew that such a beautiful setting beside Lough Mask, buried deep in the shelter of Glenbeg, Cnoc a Chorreen and Cnoc na Muice, could hold such memories for me. Never again, I vowed to myself, would I be belittled, laughed at and ridiculed. I might not always have the right words to articulate my thoughts and opinions, but I knew I could think. I knew I was good at that. I had learned the power of silence. I had learned to be unflappable, to take what was thrown at me, to digest insults, to process demeaning phrases and measure this against my own self-belief where somehow, I managed to shrug off any feelings of not being good enough. I believed in myself; I didn't care what others thought of me, and I had a strong desire to make something of myself. I left that school, driven, focused, obsessed and determined to succeed. I was never going to listen to anybody who said I couldn't do something if I thought otherwise. Those educated people had done nothing for me and I could see clearly that I had to go it alone. I wasn't angry or resentful, nothing like that. That isn't in my nature. Nobody really knew what was going on inside my head, but I knew I would make something of myself, no matter what, I just didn't know how I was going to do it.

As was expected when I finished school, I took on the man's role around the farm. My father now working with Grant Rail, was getting better work and improving his lifestyle but the money he made involved working shifts and spending longer periods away from home. This was difficult for my mother and grandfather as the farm still had to be managed. I was certainly ambitious and had been considering how I could improve things on the farm. I looked at our methods of farming and could see that we were very reliant on each other; neighbours working together to help each other out. I thought to myself that instead of being the one waiting for the farmer with the tractor to be free to help, I could be the one who had the tractor and charge people a small daily rate for its use. In that way, the people who hired me didn't have to give me a day's work in repayment and could get on with their own work. In our Parish at that time only one other person had a tractor, and he didn't hire it out at all. I knew I had a good plan. I also knew that my mother might not agree as she had strong neighbourly instincts and loved the traditions that involved giving a day's work to each other in return for help. I had no money and so had to prepare a good argument to get a loan from my mother. I had decided that I needed to purchase a grey Massey Ferguson. At sixteen, I was ready to buy a tractor to hire out to people cutting hay and turf. I knew that convincing my mother that this was a good idea was going to be tough, however, I needed to get her blessing as well as her money. I was well aware that my father sent home good money but also knew that it was hard to come by and that my mother dutifully saved every penny she could. My trump card was that I knew that she had faith in me, and she wanted me to stay at home.

Unknown to my mother, I had already gone to Ballinrobe with my neighbour Michael Anthony who travelled there to buy a car from Fahy's Garage. As Michael was finalising his deal, I spied the little grey Massey Ferguson and made my own deal with Fahy. We shook hands on a hundred and eighty pounds. I left Ballinrobe that day six inches taller, totally delighted with myself, not once considering that I had made a deal and had shaken hands on it without having a penny to my name. I was so sure my mother would help me out and indeed she did. She gave me a loan to buy my first tractor. I felt invincible. I borrowed a trailer from our neighbours, the Liams and hired myself out to any farmer who needed help. I had already established a good reputation for myself as a hard worker and with my trailer, I had a nice little business for myself. I worked very hard and made sure that nobody had cause to complain about anything. I arrived early and stayed until every single last bit of work was completed. I was constantly mulling over in my head different ways I could improve my fledgling business, so I decided to buy a plough with the intention of diversifying and getting more work. I had enough money made to buy the plough at a cost of forty-five pounds. This proved to be a shrewd move and enabled me to have resources to buy my own trailer that cost me a significant two hundred and fifteen pounds. Every time I managed to accumulate, I decided to speculate. I didn't really ever consider doing anything else with my earnings, apart from repaying my loan to my mother of course. I would earn a bit and spend a bit. I was also thinking about enlarging my fleet to include a second grey tractor when I heard that 'The Larches' public house was being built in Finney in 1968.

Breid and John Coyne had a great vision for the area. They could see the potential when they decided to build 'The Larches'. This was a significant development as there was nothing like it in our place. It caused a great excitement in the Parish. People were thinking about the social aspects, but I was calculating that the contractors would need local workers to construct the groundworks for the grand new public house, the first building to be constructed in the area in years.

After many years of economic downturn, the Coynes realised that seventies Ireland and the prospect of greater ties with Europe, would bring new hope and opportunity. They were tapping into the optimistic feel-good factor when they built 'The Larches'. They were spot on, indeed, the enjoyment this place brought to our Parish can never be underestimated.

I approached the main contractor and was thrilled to be given work. My job was to drive the tractor and machines moving the muck and so I learned loads and gained much needed experience driving machinery. This little bit of practice stood me in good stead and was a skill that I was to exaggerate much later in London. As the new building arose from the stony lakeshore road, it brought with it hope for a better future: a future that would hopefully provide employment and enable people to work at home. For my part, I was delighted to earn enough money on site to combine with my own driving work and add to my little fleet by buying a mower. I was buying bits of machinery with the money I earned. I realised that I was good at this work and felt proud of myself.

Times were changing. I had a few pounds in my pocket and so I decided that I would make a purchase unconnected with my dream of having machinery. Lough Mask is a breathtakingly beautiful scenic spot, although like most locals, I took no notice. I had become totally accustomed the splendour of the area. I would hear holiday makers talking forever about the mists sweeping down from the hills, the mayfly emerging for their one glorious day of freedom and I would simply shrug. I would see visitors delighted to sniff the sweet scent of turf and roll my eyes to heaven. All I could see was that it was mighty difficult to get out of the place without transport and at sixteen, I had an idea that life might be more wildly interesting beyond the confines of the lake. My sense of adventure was beginning to kick in and my response was to buy myself a Honda 50 from Joe Michael. It was my passport to freedom. I went all over on it, from dancing in Cong, to spins around the lake and to the pub to play cards. The world was my oyster and the card game Twenty-Five, with Anthony Joyce in Duffy's shop in Finney, was the place to be.

This was the game of choice, we spent hours playing for a pig's head which was expertly dressed by Marcus. Duffy's shop was the only place with electricity and a television at that time and therefore, a big draw for all of us on a Saturday night at six o'clock when we would all pile into their living room to watch Ironside. What a gentleman Paddy Duffy was to put up with all of us congregating in his front room!

The Honda 50 was in big demand, and I was known to lend it to my sisters, Mary, Barbara and Nóra when they wanted to go to the shop in Finney. That was until there was a knock at the door and the local garda (police) made his presence felt. It seemed he wasn't so delighted at the prospect of underage girls in his beat travelling alongside Lough Mask on a Honda 50!

There were lots of young people in the Parish then and the Honda 50 made sure I got to local dances where we would stand on one side of the hall eyeing up the ladies on the other side. We had the best of music and after a few glasses of porter we would be brave enough to take the wretched walk across the floor. What a walk it was, all eyes boring into you, wondering who you were going to ask and you wondering if they would turn you down and make you walk all the way back again to the jeering and laughing of the lads. We called it the walk of shame. We were carefree and full of life.

As I look back now and consider my late teenage self, I can see that my ambition was beginning to spur me on. I loved my life in Kilbride and had done everything possible to make a real go of it. I wasn't afraid of hard work, but I knew I wanted to work for myself and my experience at school had forged in me a strong desire to prove I could make something of myself. My family certainly believed in me and supported me, but I had a terrible need to prove to myself that I wasn't useless and good for nothing as I had been led to believe at school. Inside of me began to grow a determination that would allow me to take whatever life threw at me, mull over it, take my time and react to it in my own manner. I like to take my time, to think about things, I don't like to be rushed into a decision. I had seen too many people rush into a situation only to be sent packing, so I told myself to take it easy, keep cool and don't get too excited.

This was a time of social change. The Fianna Fail education minister, Donogh O'Malley made an unauthorised speech promising free education for all and despite the uproar, this was introduced in September 1967. This really was an historic turning point for Ireland and changed the lives of all future generations. While this was too late for me and most of my family, my younger siblings got free second level education. That has made a huge difference in Ireland. especially in rural Ireland. Some of my siblings were able to achieve professional jobs and lead lives that were far removed from the life of toil our parents experienced[2].

Michael, the second youngest of my siblings was my constant companion and able to drive the tractor when I eventually left home. He was eight years of age when he showed my father and a neighbour, Johnny Sheain Tommy, how to plough a field. Michael had half the field ploughed in the time the two men discussed how to work the tractor and plough. He was great on the tractor and great at school too. Life was different for the younger ones; it was much better.

My family at home were known as the Terrys. There were so many Flannery families in the area that it was necessary to distinguish one branch of the family from another. Somebody way back must have been called Terry, and then because it is an unusual name in the West of Ireland, we all got landed with the name. The name Terry has died out through the generations and piseog (superstition) tells us that it is now bad luck for anybody in the family to call a child Terry. Needless to say, nobody has tested this theory out! Surnames are used less frequently in Gaelic and people are referred to by their given name, followed by the name of a parent and sometimes a

---

[2] The Irish Times -lessons from history, Brian Maye

grandparent. My father therefore was known as Máirtín Terry and I would be known as Paidí Mhairtín Terry.

Mairtín Terry was an ambitious man. His ambition was to clothe us, to feed us and to provide a roof over our heads. He worked very hard for his family and encouraged us all to believe in ourselves. My self-belief in the face of extreme challenge was certainly nurtured from my home. I believed that I could achieve more than was expected of me. Now I recognise, I had a drive and ambition handed down to me by both of my parents. I knew that if I had to labour for somebody on a farm or indeed anywhere, I would certainly do it, but only for a short time. It was a means to an end; I had no interest in it. I knew I had to do something to prove I was better than everyone thought. I had my tractor, trailer, plough and bits of equipment to make myself indispensable to those around me. I was going to be the main man to go to in the Parish for tractor hire.

Opportunity comes to all of us in lots of different ways. The thing is to recognise it, seize it and give it a go. The ways that opportunities have presented themselves to me in my life have in one way been unremarkable but in another have changed everything. I can think of two such opportunities that altered my life completely and they could so easily have been missed for they appeared so insignificant.

It was one of those special days in May: The Mayfly was out in force and anglers were already positioning themselves along the rocky shore under trees, to sit quietly, waiting for the trout to begin to jump for the flies. I had always been at my happiest out on the lake where it was just myself and nature. I always loved to hear the gentle lapping of the waves against the clinker-built boat, the mist rolling in the dampness of the air and the sheer solitude. However, on this particular day, it was not fishing that was foremost on my mind, but a job I had later that day for a neighbour and something that he had said to me the previous evening. The neighbour was known as 'Man and a Half.' He was a local legend and earned his nickname because he was known in England as a great worker; he could do the job of two men, digging and laying cables. It was said that when he started to dig, he would cover so many miles digging that he had to get a bus back for his jacket that he left at his starting point.

'Man and a Half' was now home now for good after having bought a place, a bit of plant, a wheelbarrow, pick and shovel. When he approached me the previous afternoon to do the job for him, he was coming from the fair. Whether or not he regretted his decision to come home and give it a go living back in Shaunafarraghan or whether he simply had a run in with one of the locals propping up the bar below in Burkes, I don't really know, but he was in earnest as he said;

"I want to tell you something-go over to England now and don't be round here making an ass of yourself. Nobody round here has money so no matter what you do you won't earn any either.

And Stocach, make sure it is England you go to for I went to New Zealand and that country is only good for drying clothes!"

I had a lot of time for this man and as I went to work for him that day, he repeated what he had said and I knew he was right, I knew the neighbours in Kilbride and the surrounding areas had no extra money. I realised then that what he said was true, I couldn't make money at home no matter how hard I tried. Nobody had money to spare.

As was my way, I thought about this for some time, realising that the sheer truth of what 'Man and a Half' had said, was hard to argue. I could see it then, something that I hadn't considered before which was that I would never make any money if I stayed at home. Everybody in the place was in the same boat, we were all the same. My sense of place was felt so deeply. I was so connected to the hills, lake and the changes in the landscape brought about by the change of seasons that, until then, I was incapable of seeing beyond. Although my father had toiled in England all of his adult life, I had never really thought about an alternative to Kilbride and my sense of youthful optimism had blinded me to what was very obvious. It had taken my encounter with the 'Man and a Half' to provide clarity through the power of that drink of truth, uisce beatha (whiskey). For that I shall be forever grateful.

I needed to process what I saw for my thinking to make sense to me. I remembered back to the time when my aunt Nora

Flannery arrived home from America to live. It's interesting how a seemly ordinary moment from the past sometimes comes into mind to make sense of thoughts of things.

My grand aunt Nora Flannery was that great hope of the people, the returned Yank. Yanks who came back were a rare breed of individual indeed. We had all heard of how great things were in America, how it was the land of fortune and we, in some sense, benefitted from this fortune every Christmas when the parcels would arrive bearing gifts and hand me downs, that we were so glad to receive. Nora came back but unfortunately, she didn't stay long, and she really didn't expect to see what she saw. I suppose in the way that people saw things improve for themselves in America she had a notion that back at home things must be improving as well. It was in the early sixties and Nora was quite horrified to see that things were still very basic in Kilbride; she didn't expect that we still had no toilets in the house. Nora had done very well for herself in America. She owned an apartment and led a fine life but had never married. Whether she was lonely or just simply homesick I don't know, but she came back to Kilbride with trunks full of fine clothes and shiny jewellery the likes of which we had never seen before. Nora was full of joy and delighted to be home. It must have been a shock all the same to leave the bright lights of New York for the candle lit cottages of Kilbride, where time had stood still, and everything was as she had left it twenty years previously. The people around recognised that too.

"Close the door or Auntie Nora will get cold!" Maggie Burke would shout to all around her, so mindful was she of Nora's changed circumstances.

What is it I wonder about the emigrant, wishing after what was and forgetting what it was that made them get up and leave in the first place. Nora tried hard to fit in the situation in which she found herself. She sorely missed some of the niceties she had become used to. Her brother, my grandfather, or as we called him, the old fella, was called on to hire a taxi and go away with her all day to Galway. He didn't have any desire to spend a day in Galway with his sister however to keep her happy he agreed to go. He had a great day along with the taxi driver; the two of them made sure they paid a visit to every watering hole in Galway as Nora sampled what the city had to offer. On realising that my father and her driver were becoming drunk, Nora became maddened. For her, alcohol was the root of every evil, and she considered this yearning for the pub one of the reasons for the poverty she saw everywhere. I can only imagine that drive back from Galway and the atmosphere in the taxi the whole journey home. Not a month had passed when the trunk, the clothes and the jewellery were all bound for America again.

Nora had a great desire to be home; she knew the magic of the place, its people, its music. She appreciated the beauty of the lake and could see the splendour of the hills. It was of these things that she dreamed as she earned her living in New York. These were the images that provoked the sadness in her heart and longing to belong. It was this that took her home, but reality can be a cruel awakening. Reality can never compare with what the emigrant's mind has missed and then been built up over the years. That was the tragedy of Nora. She never ever returned again.

I was thinking of Nora shortly after she left as I was working out in the field. In my own way, her story tied in with what 'Man and a Half' had said earlier, that you couldn't grow rich in an area where nobody had anything to spare. I had also recently noticed a family called the Liams, in our area. They were a family returned from England for holidays, driving nice cars and talking about being big sub-contractors in England. I was always interested when I heard them talking about work over a pint in the pub, but I suppose I took more interest as I began to consider my own future in Kilbride. I would never make anything of myself if I stayed at home no matter how much I loved it. I recognised that Nora Flannery was very brave to admit to herself that she had been wrong to come back. It took courage to do that, and I knew that deep within myself, I too had courage. In bucketfuls.

Chapter 4
London Calling

With 'Man and a Half's' advice going round in my head, as well as perhaps new thoughts about how things turned out for the disappointed Nora Flannery, I knew with a great certainty that the time had come for me to spread my wings. I had made up my mind to follow the brothers, Jimmy and John. It was time to leave the little sisters, Mary, Barbara, and Nora, all of whom I could see would benefit from opportunities on offer in a changing Ireland. I knew they'd be well educated and already they were making plans for when they finished school. This fast pace of change in Ireland meant that the youngest in the family, Bridie and Michael were English speakers and their life would be totally different to that of their older siblings. My father was in his mid-forties at this stage, but was lingering on working in England, as he was making good money. I suppose it was all he knew, having married young, in his twenties but never having stayed with his family. He was probably used to living independently and it was a big disruption to his lifestyle to return, but his failing eyesight left him no choice. He had depended on me to keep things going on the farm, for although Michael was a natural farmer, he was too young to have that responsibility. It was my turn now; I was nineteen and had the world at my feet. He never said anything about the fact that me leaving would greatly impact on him and he must have expected it to happen someday. I was not for staying any longer. I had to go. I had ambition, sol had to get on with it. With hindsight, I see now of course that the loan for the grey tractor was given in the hope that I would remain on the farm and that it must have been devastating for my parents when I said I too was leaving. However, as was their way, they accepted it.

I will never forget the excitement of my first time going to London. I took down the old, battered suitcase my father had used on his journeys and thought about how life was about to change for me. I remember casting a quick look around my room, packing the clothes I had been able to buy from my earnings with the tractor and wondering what kind of an impression I was about to make in the bright lights of London. I was so tall that most of my trousers were too short and if I ever managed to get trousers long enough in the leg, they'd be way too big at the waist. I was annoyed about this and thought that surely, I would be able to get trousers to fit me in London. I was a bit concerned about going to London and this concern was not without justification. I had cajoled Barbara into helping me to learn to read the basics, enough so I could get by, and the poor girl had a terrible job trying to teach me. I kept at it though as I wasn't going to let anything stop my nineteen-year-old self from making a go of it. I was sorry to leave my grey tractor behind me, for I knew it had done me proud. I glanced around the room I shared with Michael, the candlewick bedspreads stuffed up against the flowery green wallpaper, the oversized brown wardrobe that took up far too much space in the small room and thought that Michael would be delighted to have a room of his own.

I made the journey to Shannon Airport with Anne, my brother John's wife who had been home on holiday. It was good to have somebody to accompany me as I had a nervous feeling in my stomach as we travelled along the stone-wall lined road. I had never been on a plane before and hadn't a clue what to expect. I remember arriving at the terminal and seeing lots of people hugging and crying as they said goodbye to loved ones. It was the same scene repeated many times; older, worn faces sadly looking on, waving at bright-eyed youngsters eagerly looking forward to what was about to come once they boarded the Aer Lingus flights to their futures. I had all my goodbyes said already and was glad of it. I had felt a tightening in my throat as I had hugged my mother goodbye that morning. She whispered into my ear.

"I ngan fhios don saol is fear a bheadh ann, a Phaidí", (whatever you do in life, do it quietly and for no praise) (Irish proverb)

I knew I would miss the girls. Mary was wailing that Bulgeen, our pet calf would miss me and no doubt, Barbara was delighted to give up her home schooling. Nora and Bridie had hugged me goodbye, and Michael tried his best to look grown up like father as he punched my shoulder and said he'd take care of the old grey tractor. I looked at the hubbub of the terminal with eagerness at the thought of what was to come but I made sure

I never showed any worry. I had learned to hide my feelings very effectively. Where I suppose I let my guard down a little, was when we got through to the arrivals lounge in Heathrow. I stood mesmerised at the sheer number of people before me. I gawped like a child at the vastness of the place as Anne went to freshen up. I stood at the top of the escalator inspecting the mechanics of the moving staircase all the while staring at the different kinds of people in my line of vision, I was amazed. I'd never seen the like of it before. To me, standing at the top of the escalator, it seemed as if men and women from every nation in the world were below on the wide-open ground floor. The smells hit me; the smell of Europe, Africa, America and God knows where else, stood in that arrivals hall dressed in clothes, the like of which I had never seen. Colourful African prints walked alongside long white robes, turbans and scarves. Black-robed figures whose faces couldn't be seen walked through the crowds, some others wore expensive looking Eastern silks. I just stopped and stood still, noticing how they all ignored each other, eyes down as they glided around like worker bees. I realised that nobody noticed me, nobody cared, and I was delighted. I laughed out loud with relief as Anne came back to where I stood; I don't know what she must have thought. People began shoving me sideways as I became aware that I was holding up the human traffic that was waiting to go down the escalator, enter the tunnel and become gobbled up by the underground trains. I realised in that instant that these people weren't going to notice my too-short trousers, or my accent. They wouldn't even see me or realise I was there. I was delighted.

I had arranged to stay with my brother Jimmy in Kensal Green. Jimmy had done very well for himself and, with his wife Mary, had bought a fine Victorian terraced house that had a spare room for me to stay in as their lodger. This house was a world away from any house I had ever seen. I remember it had a lovely arched doorway and turreted frontage; I felt very proud of what Jimmy had achieved. I knew I was very fortunate to have Jimmy living in London as he had achieved a lot in a short space of time. Jimmy was well known in the Irish construction scene; Kensal Green was only a short walk from the Kilburn High Road where everybody from Ireland seemed to live, so he was well placed to know what was going on. It was the late sixties, and London was swinging. It was the era of The Beatles and Abbey Road, of Mary Quant and Carnaby Street, London was the fun-loving capital of the world, but I never noticed that life at all. There was a cultural revolution going on that saw anti-nuclear protests taking place. Young people were flocking to the city. Nowadays people talk about this period in London as a time when freedom of expression saw artists, musicians, actors and creative types get together. For those of us freshly off the boat from Ireland, the swinging sixties was a Central London thing and one that didn't concern us at all. We had our West of Ireland bubble and that was all we needed or wanted.

The place to be was 'The Orange Tree' in Stonebridge. On my first night out on the town, I walked into that place with a great smile on my face as the old familiar tunes belted out on accordion and fiddle. It was a real Irish family pub with musicians from home playing constantly and children who were filled up with too many Coca Colas darted in and out of punters holding up the great, polished wood central bar. Any worry I had about my move to England left me when I walked into 'The Orange Tree'. The imposing building with its mock Tudor façade was alien to me from outside but the minute I walked through the door, I felt at home. At home, only better. Here, there were more people, there was more music and undoubtedly more craic. My clothes were as good as anyone else's, every accent from Ireland was to be found in that public house. Lads bantered with each other about County Teams, work, music and the latest news from home, all wearing suits and ties. It looked like a solicitors' convention, but that's the way it was. I loved the feel of the place, the jostling, the humour, the acknowledgement of one another and I thought to myself that this was the life for me, way better than staying at home ruminating about how I was going to make money out of nothing.

Every Friday night the roads of Kilburn and Cricklewood came alive, the shirt and tie with proper shoes made admittance to the Galtymore a certainty. Irish men who wore shabby, dirty clothes all week as they went about their daily toil, were transformed. These men were sleek and groomed every weekend. They were instantly recognisable as Irish. The same suit that graced the halls and bars of West London at the weekend could be seen standing outside Sacred Heart Church in Quex Rd every Sunday morning. We would go into Mass for a bit and then wander off outside to catch up with people from

Kerry, Donegal, Mayo and Connemara, all talking Gaelic in different dialects and having the craic. We must have been a strange sight, all the black suits every Sunday morning standing on the street corner. We took great pride in our appearance; I met nice lads and still have great friends from back then; we were all the same.

I have heard people say construction companies back in the early seventies were not looking after their own by using the pubs as a job centre and a community bank, but I don't really see it that way at all. Everyone knew that to get work, to get your cheque cashed, to hear of the next big job, there was only one place to go, the pub. It was the centre of our lives socially and economically. Lots of people didn't have a bank account and indeed couldn't open a bank account and so the pubs were the only option open to them. Looking back now I can see that this must have been hard, a temptation for some, but mostly, the pubs were providing a service. Jimmy brought me to "The Crown" in Cricklewood the first weekend I was over to meet some fellas he knew and to try to get me the start. This red sandstone building was the second home for many Irishmen at the time. If the Irishman was not to be found inside having a pint and enjoying the craic in the evening, he would certainly be outside in the morning waiting for "the call on" to get a day's work. I watched as the craic got going, it was clear that Jimmy was well thought of and that these lads he was talking to were sizing me up. As much as Jimmy tried, he didn't manage to get me the start that night at all. Whether they genuinely had nothing for me or didn't like the look of me, I don't know. We found ourselves the next morning at half past six, standing on a street corner in Willesden Green with a lot of other Irish lads. It was like a hiring fair of old. A man in a van would come up, look at us and signal to somebody to jump in or they would simply look and drive off. It was a humiliating enough experience but luckily for me, a van pulled up and Jimmy got talking to them. Inside were two fellas from Sligo and Galway, Devine and McHugh. They took their chances and decided to give me a start. Jimmy told me that they were hard to work for, that I would earn every penny I got working for them. I was nervous but I knew how to work, and I was off, my first job in England, one I will never forget.

I suppose because I was well thought of at home in terms of being a good worker and with the cockiness of youth, it never occurred to me that I wouldn't be able to complete any task set before me. Mick Devine was a burly, ruddy-faced country man who had high expectations of his workforce. He had a job to do and expected that it would be done to perfection. He told me to clean down the concrete pipe with a jackhammer which in itself was a basic enough task. The poor man had every reason to expect that I would do it right. Never having been given such a task before and not wanting to seem lacking by asking any questions, I lifted the jackhammer and hammered it down as hard as I could. I made mincemeat of the pipe, a terrible job. There was silence in the air after that, a sense of disbelief as every man on the job looked shocked at what I had done.

Devine walked over to where the shattered pipe lay, he looked at me in the eye and said, "That was my fault, young fella I thought you knew, I should have told you." In those few words I understood the power of networking. Devine knew Jimmy, and because of that and only because of that, I kept my job. It took him a long time to clean the pipe. I had made a huge mistake but not a word was said about it after that.

I was really mortified. I felt so bad about the pipe, I did everything I could to make up for it. I worked twice as hard as any other fella on site in an attempt to make up for my mistake. In me, Devine had a committed worker who was never going to take any chances ever again. I was a man who had so much to prove to himself and indeed to others around him. That was another lesson I learned from the whole sorry experience; if somebody gives you a second chance, you must do your utmost to prove that they were right to do so.

Devine and McHugh taught me so much. They were very hard workers and Jimmy was right, they expected a lot from those they employed. If you showed any interest or ability at all, which I did, there was plenty to learn. That was the way it was, every man learned on the job, and I had to show I was clever enough to keep my head down and take what was given. It was the best training any man could get. I respected these men and worked for them for a couple of years without ever repeating the error of my first day. I knew that I was improving greatly. I had a clear idea of what to do and I was becoming quite handy. I still had the notion that I was not going to labour for anyone too long and so I began to make a plan in my mind of how I would achieve my goal. The pay I was receiving was alright, but I was well aware that I had to work very hard for my wages. The banter in 'The Crown' on a Friday night about different sub-contractors made me think that I needed to find less gruelling, better paying work if I was ever going to be my own boss. I found employment with Tommy, one of the Liam's, our neighbour from back home. He offered better pay. I had it in my mind that I needed to stop labouring and get my first machine, so I eagerly accepted this new work.

Life was wonderful really. I was still living with my brother Jimmy, working hard all week to then donning my suit and tie on a Friday night to head up to 'The Crown' in Cricklewood. The Irishman had a reputation for being a good drinker, but I received a piece of very good advice from a Dublin man, Jackie Thornton, who told me to work hard all week, avoid the pubs and keep my drinking to the weekend. At that time lots of people frequented the pubs around Kilburn after work, as for many, it was preferable to going home to a lonely bedsit. The truth of the matter was that it was the ruin of many a good man too. I listened to Jackie Thornton and made sure I only drank at the weekend when the music and singing would accompany chat and laughter in every pub along the Kilburn High Rd. As the sound of craic and laughter filled the air from Monday to Thursday, I would be seen ignoring the call to enjoy the lively atmosphere of the many pubs dotted along the road. Instead, I would run from Willesden Green to Kensal Green as I was too impatient to wait for a bus. I must have looked a strange sight in my working clothes running along the road. I used to leave my boots behind in the yard ready for de-icing in the morning by stuffing lighted papers inside them.

Another piece of advice Jackie gave me was to make sure that my sandwiches only had cheese on them and not ham, he believed that there was no nourishment in ham and considered it way too expensive. It was just as well that Jimmy's wife Mary would have a warm nourishing meal ready for me every evening when I came in from work, as I'm not too sure about that particular piece of advice. I was very fortunate to have lodgings with Jimmy, Mary and their family.

It was 1969, London was the centre of the universe but for me and my generation from the West of Ireland, the 'swinging sixties' held little interest. We just didn't care for things like that. Men's fashion was changing ties, belts and lapels got wider, collars got longer and wider and a modified version of the bell bottom called "flares" became popular but yet again, we were not at all influenced by any of this. Whether this was because we felt it didn't belong to us, this popular culture, or because we genuinely didn't even realise it existed it is difficult to know. We were, in one respect living out our lives in London exactly as we would have done in Ireland. We were all together in a new land.

Being from the West of Ireland meant a lot to us and we liked to hang out with people who were the same as us. All along the Western seaboard the same polkas, reels and jigs were played, sometimes with subtle differences but they were celebrated with joy; the same songs and airs were shared and appreciated. We had a very strong sense of self; a great belief in ourselves and an ability to do well. We were hardworking during the week, and we played hard at the weekend.

On a Friday night, every bathtub in Kilburn was piping hot to clear away the grime gathered on sites all over London during the week. The Lifebuoy soap was lathered on, the Brut was splashed and the Brylcreme loaded as every Irishman climbed into his suit, shirt and tie ready to conquer Northwest London. For my own part, I had ditched the trousers I had brought from Ireland, no more for me were the too short legs or the massive waists. I had discovered that in London they knew men came in all shapes and sizes and even if like me, you didn't have the money for a tailor you could still get trousers to fit.

We felt like kings, myself, Tommy and Johnny Walsh and Jackie Thornton as we went out on the town every Friday night visiting the pubs and then rounding off our night in that great place, the 'Galtymore'. The music was just what we wanted, country and western from Margo and Big Tom and a bit of ceilidh from The Inisfree Ceilidh Band. We could have a few sandwiches there if we wanted to but mostly, we wanted to have a few more pints before we would pluck up the courage to take to the dance floor.

Every Parish in Ireland was represented, and it was in that place many a match was made. I don't know if a more humiliating way to ask a girl to dance was ever invented than the strut across the floor of the suits in the 'Galty'. It was even worse than at home. The women would sit at one side of the hall and watch as we, tanked with stout went walking, ready for the big let-down. There was much jostling, banter and craic as half drunk and full of swagger, we would eye one pretty girl and manoeuvre ourselves in what we supposed was a manly saunter across the empty floor. Half ways across, the doubt would set in, no doubt influenced by the giggles, and the whispering of the ladies on the other side as they gasped in horror at the sight of what was approaching. For us however, it was too late, we had usually gone past the point of no return, we simply had to keep going. If you got a refusal when you eventually made it to the other side and asked a girl to dance, then it was best to turn on your heel and go back. It was better to face the jeering lads than ask the next girl to dance who would surely refuse so as not to dance with somebody that her friend had already rejected.

It was a terrible thing, the refusal, but a worse thing was the lads' scorn on the other side. No wonder we needed to have a drink on us to go through it all. It mustn't have affected us too badly really because we did this every Friday and Saturday night of the year even though for us entrance was costly enough, around ten bob each.

Sunday was a day for the pub and to attend Mass; we did this in no particular order. Before Mass we used to go to the Parish Centres for a pint and after Mass, we would resume our interrupted drinking and go to the Catholic clubs where great friendships were made, drink was cheaper, and the beer was good. Sunday nights saw all of us head home early, clubs closed at half past ten, ready for the week ahead.

In 1971 when I started to work for O'Brien, I was getting three pounds a week more which brought my wages up to thirty-six pounds a week. I was managing to save twenty pounds a week and I was delighted with that. I would budget to spend a fiver on drink at the weekend, and that left me another fiver to play with, so I never felt I was struggling at all.

That first Christmas away from home, I worked until two o'clock on Christmas Eve. I had sent a card home with money as a gift and remember buying a few bottles of whiskey. It was so strange being in London for Christmas. It was bitterly cold, so we went to 'The Orange Tree' for a couple of drinks, but the bright lights and tinsel held no store for me as I hankered after family sitting around the warmth of the turf fire telling stories and playing cards. I missed the smells of home, the freshness of the air laden with the sweet scent of turf, the purple heathered hills and the gentle lapping of waves at Lough Mask. Despite the amount of music in London's Irish pubs, I missed the music in 'The Larches', I missed it all as I listlessly trailed the hard, frost-tinged footpaths back to Kensal Green and for the first time, seeds of doubt crept slowly into my dreams.

I vowed that Christmas to go home for a month in the summer, I was long enough away and was in desperate need of a bit of craic, the relentless toil for the release of the weekend was taking its toll. I was desperate to hear stories from home, I needed to reconnect, to be myself, to relax. The weeks leading up to the summer holiday were heady with excitement, and nothing could dampen my spirits. Of course, the suit to go home was bought, everyone had to have a new suit, I had to look the part of a man coming from England. I had to look successful no matter how little was in my bank account. I knew that when I was propping up the bars of Clonbur in my crisp new suit, I would be scrutinised and questioned about every single detail of my life in London. The highly awaited day came, and I was getting a lift home with my cousin Billy Murphy. We drove to Holyhead, suitcases in the back of the car. It was a long boring journey however I will never forget my first sight of Clonbur when I arrived back home for the first time. I couldn't believe how small the village looked. How had a place so small been the centre of my universe for such a long time, I wondered to myself. I stared at the neat, terraced houses and watched the old fellas chatting outside 'Burke's' like I had never seen them before. Never before had I noticed how people couldn't walk the length of the street without stopping to chat; nobody was in a hurry, I was delighted.

My family home was full as usual, everybody liked to gather there. All the neighbours would pop in to visit on their way by. Mother always had the kettle on the range ready to hand out a steaming cup of tea to any weary traveller and my father was great for talking. The old Traveller, Johnny Maughan was a regular visitor, parking his caravan up the road as he peddled his tin wares. My father and Johnny would often be sat either side of the fire sharing stories and so it was as I returned home that day. There was no great show of emotion for me as the returned son but as my father looked up at me and told Johnny about how all of his sons were doing in England, I could see pride in his eyes and that was all I needed to see. Mother, on the other hand, showed her love with food. Five minutes after my arrival the table was full and the younger ones were looking for attention as everyone wanted to talk to me, the returned emigrant.

That night I went to 'The Larches', and it was great to have the bit of sterling in my pocket; sterling was king. I had plenty of money and plenty of time to enjoy myself. There was always a crowd around, Paddy Andrew and Aggie, Mairtín Phateen, Nuke and Máirtín Sonny were nearly always there, and Liam Mulroe was to be found in behind the bar telling jokes and regaling us with stories as John Coyne the owner, walked around chatting to everyone. I went out every night of the week and indeed at the weekend too. Life in Kilbride was brilliant that summer of 1971. I still had my old grey tractor at home and as I had so much time on my hands, I made sure I put it to good use and spent my time cutting hay and working for a few farmers to enhance my holiday spending money. Brendan Shine was number 1 with 'O'Brien has no place to go', the troubles in the North were heating up, the Irish Women's Liberation Movement was after travelling from Dublin to Belfast on a women's rights protest; things were certainly changing. For places like Kilbride however, change was at a slow pace. Kilbride remained relatively untouched by the outside world. I was in my element being back at home but of course I knew it couldn't last.

Saving hay with my father, Jimmy & John

Father and his children, Mary, Barbara, Jimmy and Paddy on top of the stack.

Julia, Bridie, Michael, Paddy, Mairtín

Nora, Barbara, Michael, Paddy

Bridie

Bridie & Michael

Julia, Mc Andrew, Paddy with
McAndrew's relatives

Michael on accordion, Paddy on Honda 50

Mairtín Flannery

Mc Andrew's car in Kilbride

Granny & Bridie

My father, Jimmy, John and Paddy

Mary's communion

Paddy on accordion

Paddy & Tommy Welsh

Barbara, Mary, Paddy cousin Mairtin, Nóra and Michael

Holland Rd.

The old school garden

The returned Yank

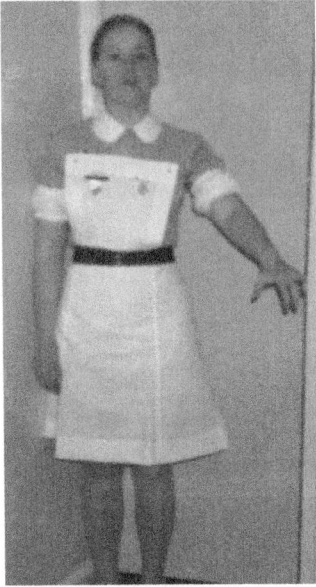

Nurse Mary Philbin

London shopping and new clothes that fit!

Mary & Paddy with friends

Mary & Paddy with friends

Martin, Paddy, Patrick & Paul

Patrick, Martin, Maria, Paul, Mary, Julia, Paddy

Mary and Paddy signing the Freedom of the City entry book

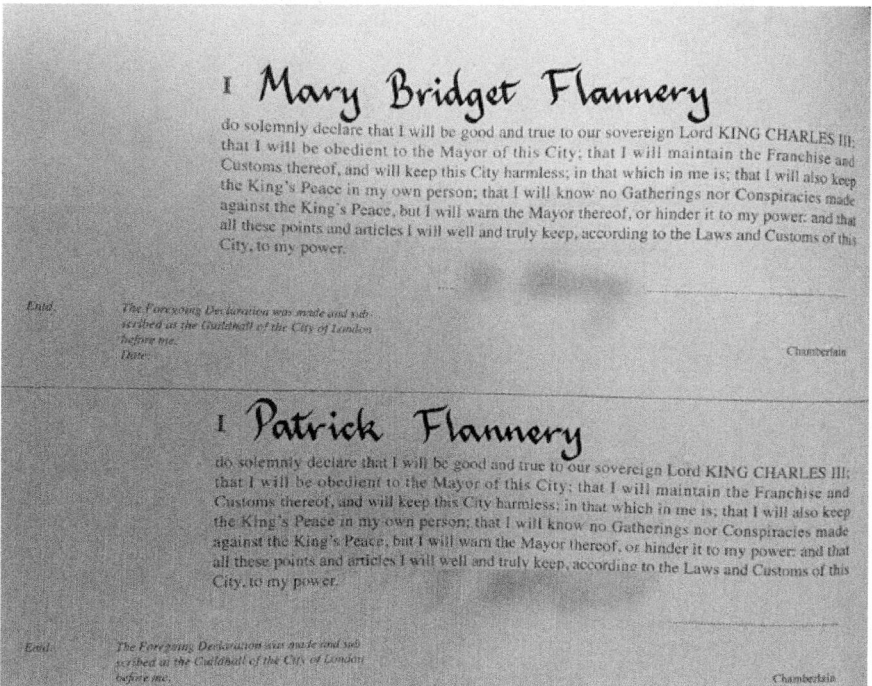

I **Mary Bridget Flannery**

do solemnly declare that I will be good and true to our sovereign Lord KING CHARLES III; that I will be obedient to the Mayor of this City; that I will maintain the Franchise and Customs thereof, and will keep this City harmless; in that which in me is; that I will also keep the King's Peace in my own person; that I will know no Gatherings nor Conspiracies made against the King's Peace, but I will warn the Mayor thereof, or hinder it to my power; and that all these points and articles I will well and truly keep, according to the Laws and Customs of this City, to my power.

Entd.   The Foregoing Declaration was made and sub-
          scribed at the Guildhall of the City of London
          before me.
          Date: Chamberlain

I **Patrick Flannery**

do solemnly declare that I will be good and true to our sovereign Lord KING CHARLES III; that I will be obedient to the Mayor of this City; that I will maintain the Franchise and Customs thereof, and will keep this City harmless; in that which in me is; that I will also keep the King's Peace in my own person; that I will know no Gatherings nor Conspiracies made against the King's Peace, but I will warn the Mayor thereof, or hinder it to my power; and that all these points and articles I will well and truly keep, according to the Laws and Customs of this City, to my power.

Entd.   The Foregoing Declaration was made and sub-
          scribed at the Guildhall of the City of London
          before me.
                                                                   Chamberlain

Paul, Mary, Paddy, Julia, Martin

Receiving the freedom of the city

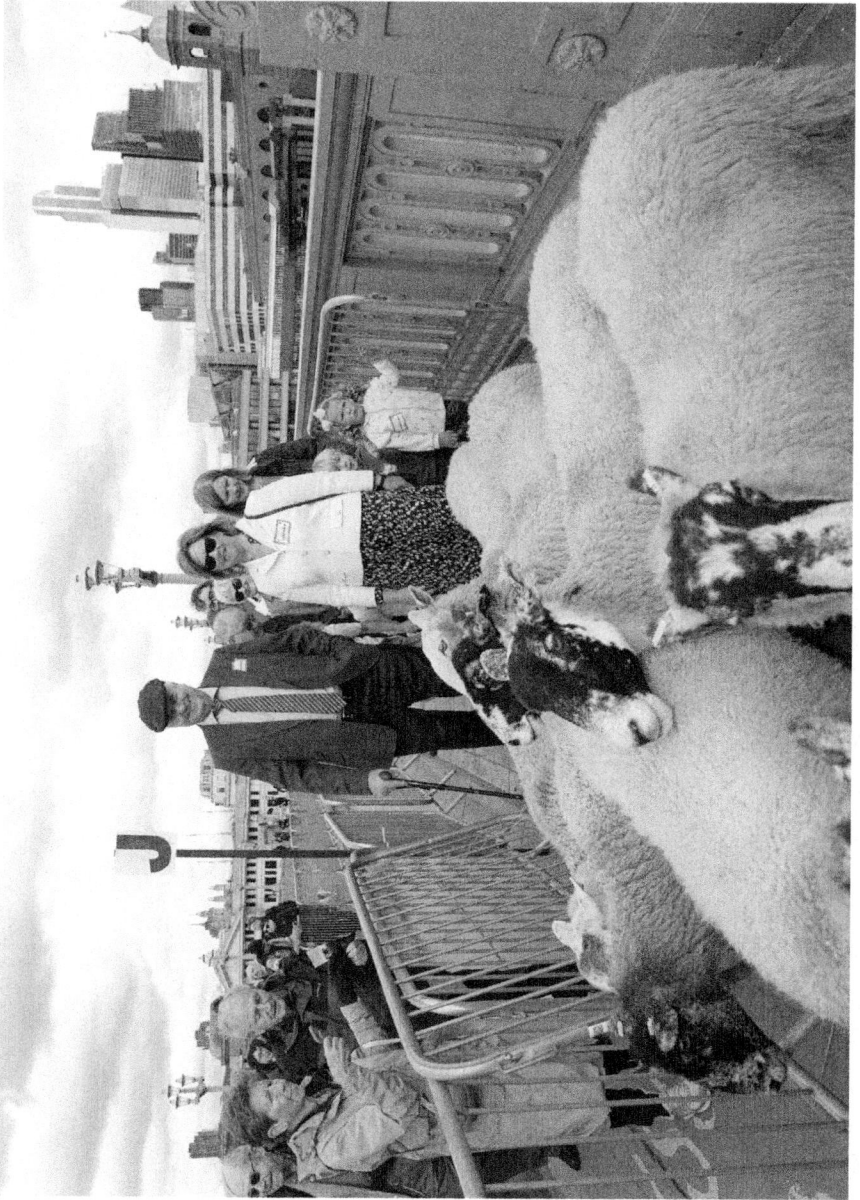

Paddy and Mary driving their flock of sheep across Southwark Bridge

The Flannery clan with Paddy on the occasion of Paddy using his freedom to drive his flock across Southwark Bridge

Grandchildren with Paddy & Mary - Isobel, Martin, Olivia, Edie, Thomas, Arthur, Molly, Conor, Grace, Tilly, Florence, Arthur

Chapter 5
Chance Meetings

I wonder how many times in our lives we meet somebody and only later realise the importance of that meeting on the rest of our lives. I also think of how many times we pass an opportunity by without giving it a second thought. Some people think that nothing happens without a reason and there is no such thing as a coincidence. I'm not sure about that, it may very well be true, I don't know, but what I do know is that my chance meeting with a man called Michael McAndrew certainly changed my life and had me thinking about things differently, just as the comment from the 'Man and a Half' had done some years before that.

I had come back to London after the summer of 1971. I was more determined than ever to make something of myself having tasted the fine life of a man with a few bob in his pocket during those long summer days. I was restless and always on the move looking for better work and better pay. The construction industry in London was booming and as I laboured on site, I used to look enviously at the machine drivers. I knew I would much prefer their work; I knew it would suit me much more. Although I shouldn't have, I jumped on a machine every chance I got. I was desperate to learn how to drive them properly. In hindsight, I must have been very annoying to work with. Tommy Welsh had managed to get me the start with a contractor called Black Mick Joyce. I wasn't doing what I was being paid to do.

They got so fed up with me that in the end I was sacked. I was becoming impatient, too cocky really, I had my mind on other things. Tommy always credits himself with helping me to be in the right place the day I bumped into Michael McAndrew. I personally claim all the credit for my fall from grace. I truly deserved it.

McAndrew was vaguely known to me through Jimmy. I had arrived back to Jimmy's house feeling a bit fed up with being asked to leave the machines alone. Tommy had given the gaffer a great reference telling him how good I was working during the construction of 'The Larches' but it was clear my machine driving ability was not good enough. I felt annoyed with myself because I had let myself get into a bad situation. It wasn't the end of the world, but my pride was dented.

McAndrew was a great man to make a situation work for him, he heard how I was fed up and wasn't keen to go labouring so a plan was hatched. I agreed to drive McAndrew and his wife around the religious sites of Europe on a three-week holiday. I found out that their driver had let them down at the last minute and McAndrew's wife wanted to complete her pilgrimages at Easter. The deal was done, and I was to be off within the week. The only problem was, unbeknown to McAndrew, I had no passport and was too young to have a driving licence, but I wasn't going to let that stop me.

While I in no way advocate law breaking as a general rule and can wholeheartedly see the foolishness of my actions, I must admit to having in my possession a passport and driving licence when the European trip was due to begin the following week. I remember it clearly; I got a map of Europe from the local garage and checked out the route that McAndrew had marked out. We planned to take the ferry from Southampton to Bilbao, visit Barcelona, Madrid, Granada and Seville in Spain before crossing over to the Portuguese Algarve, dropping in on Fatima on the way to Lisbon and Porto. From Porto we planned to cross over the Spanish border to Finisterre and travel up to San Sebastian. After that we would cross the Pyrenees and stop off in Lourdes. From Lourdes we intended to visit La Rochelle and drive up to Paris before departing for England from Dieppe. Elizabeth McAndrew wanted to visit Fatima, Lourdes and a host of lesser-known Catholic places of worship on the trip. McAndrew himself didn't seem too bothered where he went or what route was taken as long as it consisted of plenty of opportunities for fine dining and wine tasting. I took full advantage of the experience. As we intended to be gone for three weeks to a month, I thought that we should try to limit driving to around 400 km per day. The McAndrews had provided a list of the cities that were of particular interest to them and so remarkable as it seems, I was the chauffeur for this magnificent road trip of religious places of interest around the Iberian Peninsula and back up through France. The names of the cities didn't mean anything to me, they were just names on a map, places I had never heard of and names I couldn't pronounce. I was nervous, but the prospect of driving the beautiful Wolseley 6 automatic car with its leather seats and walnut dash made my day and got rid of any negative thoughts from my head. It was a beautiful car, and I was delighted to be behind the wheel.

Approaching Southampton, I eyed the MS Patricia with a feeling of unease knowing it was to be my home for the next twenty-four hours. It was not as bad as I feared, I had heard that the crossing was quite rough and very boring, but our journey was calm, and I had a cabin I had to share with a stranger. I didn't mind that one bit as long as it wasn't too rough. Initially the boat was full of excited passengers ready to begin the journey to the continent. However a couple of hours around the seemingly never-ending Bay of Biscay soon quietened the chatter and the air became pungent with the smells of spilled tea and stale human sweat. There was little opportunity for small talk on this wearisome journey and this suited me well as I am not somebody who likes to engage in chit chat, and I think that it also suited both of the McAndrews too.

We were delighted to see the port of Bilbao looming in the distance and excited for the next leg of the journey along winding country roads to Zaragoza, a famous pilgrimage site where Our Lady is said to have appeared before her Assumption into Heaven. Along that route, dotted with clay-coloured villages, I found out that McAndrew had gone to Trinity College Dublin to study medicine but had become fed up with his choice and came to England rather than finishing his studies. Much to his family's dismay, he had been tempted by the post war boom in construction and the prospect of making money. Elizabeth McAndrew, who was also Irish, from County Carlow, had qualified as a home economics teacher and met her husband in London. The couple had been married for years but had no children. Perhaps this was part of the reason for the pilgrimage, but if it was, it was certainly not discussed. McAndrew was not as devout as his wife but was very happy to accompany her to places of worship. I, in turn, was also expected to partake in this religious observance. While the trip was planned around places of apparition and churches, it was also planned around vineyards and the culture to be enjoyed in the various cities along the route. McAndrew was small in stature and because he loved fine dining, a bit overweight. I was no foodie at that stage. However, along with his elegant wife Elizabeth, I began my journey of discovery through the splendid restaurants of France, Spain and Portugal. In Barcelona, I sampled tapas; in Madrid I ate venison; in Seville, with its orange groves I had the juiciest fruit I had ever tasted. I tasted escargot in La Rochelle and duck in Santiago de Compostela; food that I had never before tasted in my life. Looking back, I was quite adventurous and tried everything, considering my staple diet up to that point had been potatoes and pork or fish. I loved the tastes and enjoyed fine food and drink all paid for by my generous employer. Mind you, I would have been just as happy with a bowl of lovely floury potatoes. It was probably on this trip too that I developed a taste for wine, a drink I took to readily having only drank beer or porter before that. We visited the vineyards of each country we passed through and stayed in lovely hotels. In Barcelona we saw the Black Madonna of Monserrat, had cold beers in the gothic quarter and admired Gaudi's La Sagrada Familia. Although I must confess, there were many times I would have preferred to sit outside the cafes drinking cold beer, I never did, as I realised then how fortunate I was to be on such a road trip. I tried very hard not to show anything but enthusiasm for the cathedrals, murals and grottos we came across. In Spain, we must have visited every Catholic shrine known to man. I really enjoyed driving through the beautiful lavender filled countryside, seeing how the landscape changed as we moved from urban Seville across to the pretty white Algarve villages. It was a fine trip and what I lacked in knowledge of the continent I made up for in my knowledge of vehicle maintenance and my driving ability even if it was on the opposite side of the road. I suppose having me as mechanic and driver provided some security for the couple. We took part in candlelit processions in Fatima and travelled on our knees to the basilica like all pilgrims do. We walked some of the Camino de Santiago in Northwest Spain and prayed at all manner of little wells and grottos dotted around the coast. As we crossed the Pyrenees, and I took in the wonder of the landscape I felt like I was in another world where I didn't belong. I had a notion that I was looking at life from the outside, such was my difficulty in believing my good fortune. The splendour of the cathedrals and the vast sizes of these places that housed paintings by famous artists I had never heard of, certainly opened my eyes to an unknown world. The crowds of pilgrims in Lourdes on candlelit procession to the healing waters of the grotto was astonishing to me. I took part and quietly said a prayer for my family at home. I bought a plastic bottle in the shape of Our Lady and filled it with holy water to take back to my mother. All of the travelling, the exposure to fine hotels, the wonderful meals and visiting magnificent places such as the vineyards was for the McAndrews, a normal holiday experience. For me, it was like being part of a world I had never even dreamed existed. I didn't mind all of the praying, or even looking at the ornate churches, even though they held no particular interest to me, as I was on an adventure I could only have imagined. The vineyards of Bordeaux saw us load the car with more bottles of "not so holy" water, we admired the magnificent châteaux of the Loire region, and eventually the rural landscape gave way to suburbs as the great city of Paris appeared in the distance. I had time to think, to consider. I had seen a land a world away from the hills of Kilbride where even the Atlantic took on a different colour in the early summer sunlight. The trip had opened my eyes to possibilities that I could never have imagined. I saw how it was possible to live. I was a changed man as we boarded the ferry home in Dieppe, and I had the McAndrews to thank for it.

Safe to say McAndrew knew my character pretty well when we had finished that trip. He knew I was a risk taker; he knew I was determined and ambitious man. He knew I was in possession of a certain assuredness that would allow me to assert my credentials and gain a driving job for him even though I had never set eyes on the continent in my life, never mind driven anyone, ever. He knew I could keep my counsel as he observed me praying at every Marian shrine we stumbled across, like a mad monk, I offered no opinion or resistance. He knew I would take risks with food, with drink, with travel, and even though I don't believe he knew the extent of my reading difficulties in English, he must have realised I was bluffing as I pretended to read menus in Spanish, French or Portuguese.

McAndrew was one of a breed of Irishmen who had recognised the need of the men from Connemara, Donegal, Mayo, Tipperary and Kerry who were much better practically than filling in forms and keeping on top of paperwork. Lots of people in those days believed that all that was needed to succeed in the UK was brawn not brain. McAndrew was the brainpower needed for brawn to succeed. This work of filling forms, obtaining bank accounts, paying taxes for many Irish firms meant that he was needed by lots of construction firms. This of course gave him a fine lifestyle which was, because of Elizabeth, also very religious. Over the years he had developed contacts within the construction industry and had established his own consultancy firm, Oval, providing accountancy for Irish companies. Oval was the name chosen because he lived next to Oval Cricket Ground.

McAndrew decided to take a chance on me and at the end of our European Grand Tour and he made me an offer. During the trip, I had explained to McAndrew that my goal was to buy a machine and that I was saving up to do just that. McAndrew had contacts within the construction industry. Wimpey was a big construction firm and a friend of his called Peter Heir was becoming fed up with the difficulties he was experiencing procuring drivers for their plant. He was just about to venture into the business of direct hire. McAndrew knew about this and so he phoned me one evening, he told me to buy a machine. He explained that he had a contract for me. I was amazed at first; a bit wary and finding his proposition difficult to grasp. I remember stammering that I had just two thousand pounds saved, far off the five thousand pounds I knew I needed. McAndrew explained that the machine would cost five thousand two hundred pounds. He would be my guarantor for a loan and charge me ten percent of my turnover. The day rate from Wimpey would be low but it would be consistent and guaranteed. My heart was racing as he explained that JCB would lend me the money and I would put down my deposit of two thousand. I don't know how I slept that night. I was in no doubt that I was going to do this but to go from having two thousand pounds saved before the holiday to owning my own machine after the holiday was to me too good to be true. Not once did I consider that I might have been paying too much; not once did I wonder at the lack of a contract or paperwork; not once did I think about my total ignorance regarding invoicing, such was my ambition to own my own machine. Wimpey knew what they were doing. They needed young ambitious lads like me who would work for one seventy-five an hour with the occasional bonus thrown in.

I was on cloud nine at the thought of owning my own machine. In my head I had costed the time it would take to make the machine pay for itself; the hours I would need to put in and I knew I was up for it and ready for the chance.

A strange thing happened a year after we got back from our road trip. McAndrew called by Jimmy's house one evening and handed me a photo of myself. Confused, I looked at him and saw that he had a wad of photographs of me. He explained with a grin that he was walking by a new photographer's shop that had just opened up near the Oval when he saw a huge photo of me in the window. Puzzled, he had gone in to find out why my photo had pride of place in their window display. He was told that a year ago, when they just opened, I had been one of their first customers looking to have my passport photo taken. McAndrew knew that I had used it to fake my road trip documents. But to give him his due, he said no more, he simply gave me copies of my photo to send home to my parents. I still have the photo he gave me hanging in my home to this day.

I was on my way. I was full of excitement and expectation as I arrived at Breakspear Road., Ruislip on that Monday morning, in June 1972. I had an added bounce to my step as I walked up to the site. There it was, my first JCB. Gleaming yellow, standing proud surveying all around. The site was busy, men bustled all around. Foremen were shouting orders as new houses emerged from the London clay. I didn't take any notice of anything else but the machine. It was mine; all of my dreams and ambition wrapped up in one grand old dame who I would make sure was ready to work her socks off for me. In this machine, my dreams would be realised. In this machine, my apprenticeship with my beautiful, old grey tractor back in Kilbride would be put to good use. I was a man of substance, a man of the moment, I was a man going places. I was Paddy Flannery. The only problem I had was that I no idea how to drive my beautiful machine. As the old saying goes, I had all the gear but no idea.

Sure, I thought to myself, how hard can it be? I had plenty practice back at home driving the old grey tractor, and indeed, I reasoned to myself, wasn't I in great demand every time I went home? I swallowed hard, looked around me at the men on site who had their heads down ignoring me and were carrying out their duties to begin their days work. They didn't even acknowledge me as I tried to look like I knew what I was doing and walked what I hoped was a most confident stride across to where my machine presided.

A brief word, before I got to where my machine lay, left me in no doubt that the lack of a welcome was not in my imagination at all. The men were in fact all having a good look at the young fella who had his own machine. A gruff looking middle-aged man whose rake thin body hid his strength, stopped me. With a toothless grin, he asked me in soft Welsh tones that didn't quite match his menacing stare, if I was the replacement for his very good mate from back up North, Keith. I was informed that Keith was driving a machine on site last week, a terrific driver by all accounts but was given his marching orders at the end of the week on account of a new system of driver owners Wimpey had established. I looked at him, shrugged, squared myself up and responded with as much confidence as I could manage. I knew nobody called Keith and had just been told to report to site.

The sense of doom I felt after that encounter and before I even reached my machine left me feeling terrified. Here I was, a stranger on site, a total imposter, who had by all accounts taken the job off a good man. I was a man who had just chanced to borrow and scrape to buy a machine and now found myself to be the 'face of the future' for the new Wimpey regime. I knew then without a doubt that I had everything to prove to them.

I collected my key, climbed into the cab, switched on the ignition and started to go to work. I was useless. It took me twice as long as it should to clear any muck away. I hadn't a clue how to operate the machine properly, but I watched. I was now the one keeping my head down and said nothing. I made many mistakes over the next few days, and it took me a month to be able to drive the machine in any competent manner at all. The men looked at me with annoyance. They were impatient and looked down on me and indeed, I couldn't blame them. I was so bad. I could hear them shouting at the agent to get somebody who could drive; that I was costing them time and effort. I pretended not to hear, which was difficult, I knew they had a point, but I had to ignore the jibes and jeers and get on with it as best I could. I was good at taking insults, without letting them get to me even though I knew they had good reason to be annoyed.

The agent though, he had to make this new regime work, he had no choice. Wimpey had dictated that this was how things would be in future, and it was in his best interests to see this new driver-owner and cheap labour strategy fulfilled. Luckily for me, the sub agents were Castlebar people, and they definitely noticed my predicament. They could see I was a young lad having a go and felt sorry for me. They helped me to learn what to do. I was a fast learner; I had to be. I was also cheap labour, and they knew it. That didn't matter so much for me. I saw it as a means to an end and although it wasn't great money, it was a fair price. Wimpey paid my expenses, provided oil and diesel and maintained my machine. I couldn't complain.

As time passed, I improved enough not to have insults thrown in my direction every day. My manner of keeping quiet in some way must have impressed the workers and I began to have banter with them as I arrived on site each morning. I was never a great man for getting involved in site politics and I must have been focusing so hard on my improving machine driving skills that I had not noticed one of the site traditions take place every Friday. It had to be spelled out to me very clearly that each Friday there was an expectation that I would provide, out of my own wages, five pounds to buy the foreman and the agent a drink. I was shocked to say the least. I knew that they were earning more than me and yet because I was an owner-driver,

I had to pay up. To me it was an awful lot of money. I was earning one seventy-five an hour and it really didn't leave me with any spare cash after I had paid my loan off, paid my ten percent to McAndrew and then paid my lodgings and travel. However, I had no choice. If I wanted to succeed, I would have to do it. So, I did.

My machine driving skills improved steadily. I was feeling more confident and becoming good enough to be awarded a standard bonus of five pounds a week. I look back now at my time in Breakspear Road with fondness and consider that to have been my training school in terms of machine driving, but more importantly, in terms of site politics. To them I suppose I was a quiet lad. They could probably see I was ambitious, and they definitely knew I was a risk taker or a 'chancer'. They could see that I worked very hard and never reacted impulsively. Perhaps they thought I was a walk over at first, somebody who was easy to get rid of, but I like to think that in me they saw determination and somebody who could accept his own failings. I looked with admiration at the genuine lads on site who worked hard each day as I had done when I was labouring. I admired their skill and something that I never had; their contentment in the knowledge that they had done a good day's work. I could see how the foremen and agent had a position of superiority and that the drinks money each Friday evening was a way of keeping in with them and making sure the following week would be successful. I now realised this was regular practice on every site. In fact they looked out for the workers. I could see that the foremen were also good men who were satisfied with the way things were.

I soon realised that I didn't have enough money left at the end of each week to make a difference to my life and I knew things were not about to change for me any time soon as it would take me forever to pay back my loans. I worked tirelessly and was eager to take on overtime as I could see how much my driving was improving. I never missed a shift and so my bonus increased. There was an issue with drivers not turning up to work which was affecting costs due to downtime, so I made sure I was there for every opportunity day or night. Even after working a shift I made myself available travelling to other sites if needed. I was hungry for work, and I wanted everyone to know it.

Chapter 6
Settling Down

It wasn't that I was unhappy with how things were going. I was delighted to have my machine. I was getting on much better on the site both with the men and the agents. I was working hard and had become quite a good driver in the process. I wasn't too happy to leave it at that. However, I was constantly working overtime and felt that the rewards weren't quite there. I could see that I needed to expand my horizons but wasn't quite sure how to achieve this aim. I did my best to make a good impression and was rewarded in 1973 when I was approached by Wimpey and asked to buy and run another machine. This was exactly what I wanted to do so I made another deal with McAndrew, who charged ten percent of income made and who was obviously delighted to be involved.

I became the proud owner of my second machine that was worth five thousand four hundred pounds. I could see that I was paying a lot to McAndrew for the loans and his invoicing, but I was not somebody who could go to a bank for a loan. I was lucky to have McAndrew, I had no choice if I wanted to fulfil my dreams. The banks would laugh me out of it if I approached them. I knew I had to be the person who was working making money for others if I was going to make anything for myself.

Edward Heath's Britain of 1973 was going through a stormy period; the miners were on strike, there were power cuts, and the three-day working week was introduced to conserve electricity in the aftermath of yet another oil crisis. Economic growth was weak and an easy money policy to improve employment was introduced. For those in the know like McAndrew, loans were readily available. The fact that this policy would be responsible for high inflation and that this might have a bad effect on my fledgling business, was not lost on me. I knew it was risky, but it was a risk I was prepared to take. The fact was that I had nothing to lose, I started with nothing and if I ended up with nothing, well then, I'd be no worse off than I was before and I knew I could always have another go. This kind of thinking spurred me on and meant that I was not overly concerned.

I now had a second machine and needed a driver who was dependable and efficient. I needed somebody who would work hard and could understand what was going on. There were things that had to be put up with on site such as the put downs, the banter, the drinks money tradition and I needed somebody who would put their head down and ignore the slight injustices. I needed somebody who was hungry to succeed, who saw themselves as a driver-owner eventually, when the chance presented. I approached Tommy Walsh. Tommy was dependable, hardworking and could put up with whatever was thrown at him on site. He was delighted for the opportunity and so both of us worked together very successfully on those early Wimpey jobs.

Tommy and I decided that because we were working together, we would rent a house together in Tooting and I have very fond memories of our time there. We were making a name for ourselves as being reliable and trustworthy which helped us get work. It was my first time not living with my family and although I was extremely grateful to Jimmy and Mary for all they had done for me, I was delighted to be out on my own and began to sort out a life for myself as a young man about town. I'm not saying that I suddenly became engrossed in the lively London scene. I continued to go to 'The Orange Tree' and other pubs to enjoy the traditional Irish music and meet up with folk from home. Although I knew I wasn't a fine musician, I always loved to play the accordion and would seek out music sessions every weekend where I could listen to others who had greater mastery, brilliant players. The Irish music scene at that time in London was in full swing. We had great players from all over Ireland, I particularly loved the music of North Connacht and could sit for hours listening to those tunes. Before he emigrated to Australia in 1972, I loved to hear Jimmy Philbin from Cornamona play. He listened to and learned from John Carty and Finbarr Dwyer, both brilliant musicians whose music transported the crowds back to their families, the hills, glens and bogs of Ireland. Jimmy was self-taught. His shyness meant that we had to stay on until the pub was closing to hear him before he picked up the box. His raw playing was of the heart, emotional and from a place deep inside. I overheard him say to John one night,

"Heaven couldn't be any better than this is Johnny; a cigarette in one hand, a pint in the other and Finbarr Dwyer playing the box."

And he meant it, every word. I was also a self-taught accordion player, the result of listening to the many kitchen sessions held at home. I couldn't read music but had a good ear and was able to pick out tunes on the accordion or as we called it, the box. I also loved the banjo and was determined to try to master it too. So, by listening to the tunes every weekend and memorising the airs I began to work on learning the banjo. It took hours; every evening after work I would pick up my accordion to play the air I was trying to perfect and then I would attempt to pick out the relevant chords on the banjo. It was a difficult task but one I thoroughly enjoyed. This was how I had learned the accordion; I would pick out easy tunes and do my best to find the chords to play. It was a great pastime for me after my hard day's work. However, I cannot say that the grumpy Scottish man living downstairs appreciated my efforts in the least. As I worked my way through the tunes, the banging on the floor would begin as he stumbled home from the pub around eleven o'clock. The Scottish man never spoke to us at all during the day; he completely ignored us. But, as he always had a good drink on him every night, in darkness it was a different story. It was then he started to scream and shout at us through the ceiling, calling myself and Tommy every description of terrible Irish name you could possibly imagine. Not that it bothered us in the slightest. We would laugh, and I knew it was time to put the instruments away for the night.

This carried on for some time; the insults grew worse, and it became apparent that Tommy, with his long hair and generally more fashionable appearance, was the prime suspect for the squealing banjo player in the Scottish man's eyes. I suppose my hairstyle had never changed since the day I left home, and my clothes were picked to fit my frame rather than because they were the latest fashion. I was in every way the same Mayo man that had arrived over a few years previously. I certainly didn't look like a hippie, or a folk singer or indeed a budding banjo player!   The Scottish man's ranting included references to hairstyle, flares, wide lapels and general appearance, in his range of insults. When I knew for certain that he thought it was Tommy playing the banjo, I must admit to finding the whole thing hilarious.

One morning however at around three o'clock there was a loud clashing sound followed by the music of 'The Pipes and Drums and the Military band of the Royal Scots Dragon Guards' as they blasted out 'Amazing Grace' just outside our door. It woke both of us up with a jolt. We were usually up around five thirty to begin our day and travel to site so we were astounded to hear the racket which appeared to come from right outside. I got up; it was still dark and freezing cold; my breath could be seen in the night air as I creaked open the door and stumbled over a huge tape recorder switched on to full volume, placed dangerously on the step outside. I looked at it, shrugged, turned it off and headed back into our room. I couldn't be bothered with his nonsense.

As I turned around to go back into the room, I was confronted by a raging Tommy, red-faced with anger at being woken up two hours before he had to get up. Before I could say anything, he had stormed out of the room, without realising the source of the noise, and tripped over the tape deck and went hurtling down the stairs on top of the waiting Scotsman, who was hunkered at the bottom to watch our reaction. There was a thud, accompanied by a roar. Tommy landed on top of him, grappled him and both of them proceeded to knock hell out of each other, all the while the Scottish man shouting about long-haired banjo folk players destroying his life.

I had no option but to go down and break up the fight and own up to the fact that he had the wrong man. It wasn't the long-haired fashionable Tommy at all who was the culprit but the short-haired, unassuming, big fella. The Scottish man was too consumed with alcohol and anger to listen to me. As far as he was concerned it was Tommy who had been playing the banjo, and nothing would deter him from this belief. As I glanced at Tommy's bloody nose and torn clothes, I must admit to feeling glad that I didn't quite look the part.

Tommy and I lived in Tooting together, from 1971 to 1972. Even though I really enjoyed my time there, I was saving up a bit of money to buy my own house. I didn't really have any idea where I wanted to buy my house, I just knew I wanted one. It seemed to be the next logical step and because I needed to sort out a loan, I entered once more into more negotiations with McAndrew. He told me that he knew of a house that somebody needed to sell in Tottenham. He arranged a mortgage and negotiated a deal for me to buy the house in Scales Rd., Tottenham. I was delighted to be a homeowner of this Victorian terraced property with three bedrooms and an outside toilet. I could play music all night long without disturbing anybody, I could come and go as I pleased. I didn't mind about the toilet being outside; I was well used to that. Tommy didn't want to move with me, he much preferred to stay in the Tooting area where he had lots of friends. I could see his point as neither of us knew the pubs around Tottenham, we had no friends living there. But having my own place spurred me on and I was happy to strike out on my own.

I suppose to McAndrew I was a dream client; I was always ready to take on risk, take on another loan and agree to the terms offered. I knew that no bank would take me on as a customer. I was still too much of a risk. I had no credit rating and lacked paperwork, including a business plan; I would never have been able to grow my business if I had not borrowed from McAndrew. It was a win-win situation. I knew he was expensive, but we forged a good relationship built on mutual understanding and respect. I was becoming a regular fixture at his elegant town house at the Oval where Elizabeth, being a terrific cook, prepared delicious meals; I was always very eager to visit.

Although I travelled home twice a year, I knew where I wanted to be. Life was good in London. I had two machines working for me, my own house and a good social life even though I had to cross London to meet friends.

I made sure that I didn't miss out on what the younger ones back home were doing with their lives. In an age where we didn't have the phone at home or regular communication, it was very easy to become a distant memory, and I didn't want that to happen.

My sister Mary was training to be a teacher in Galway. She was becoming quite the woman about town. I was amazed to see how quickly she and the younger ones were growing up. Things were getting better; more of the family were working and therefore money was more plentiful. Mary was full of fun and generally spent every penny she earned, so much so that she and her friends regularly ran out of food. Ever resourceful, they knew that a local girl, Mary Philbin from Cornamona, also working in Galway, cooked a stew for herself on a Monday with the intention of making it last until Thursday. Mary squealed with laughter as she told me that they made sure to pay her a weekly visit. Invariably, the stew was demolished by my famished sister and her friends who thought that Mary Philbin, with her tasty stew was a great find. I was delighted to see how well Mary was doing and made sure herself and Barbara, who was also training to become a teacher, came to stay with me in London during the school holidays to earn extra money.

During Christmas of 1972, I had gone home as usual. My head was full of yet another proposition McAndrew had made to me to purchase a third machine. I was mulling it over; I could see how this would really help me pay off loans quicker and I was thinking that I could use some of my savings towards the machine, reducing the amount I had to borrow. It was a move I really wanted to make and needed to think about carefully over the holidays.

As was my usual practice each time I went home, I headed up to 'The Larches' where I knew I would meet Mairtín and Johnny Sonny. My memory of that Christmas is very clear in my mind. The place was packed, steamy with cigarette smoke, streamers hung from every corner, live music played in the corner interrupted by occasional bursts of singing, lights twinkled, and it seemed as if everyone for miles around was in 'The Larches'. There was an air of excitement as we greeted each other again after so many journeys off to different parts of Ireland, America and England. Everyone was dressed in the latest fashions and some, not all, loved showing off their new clothes from London, Manchester, Birmingham, Galway and Dublin. It was great to swap stories about work, life, new friends but even better to see everyone again. Nothing had changed, but in a way everything had changed.

Generally, most people back in those days were delighted to be home. Some loved their new lives far away, released from the loneliness of rural Ireland; others breathed a sigh of relief to hear the local dialect again, hear the local tunes, sing local songs, and live a totally different way of life from their adopted cities even if only for a holiday. The sad songs of emigration were belted out, as were local songs of loss such as Striopal Cill Bhríde, a song about the loss of families during the land commission moves. Some people ordered Babysham to show how cosmopolitan they had become while others were content with porter.

Stripáil Chill Bhríde
'Séard' a dúirt Mamaí Walsh, Á mbeadh sé dírithe
'S na ballaí deanta' Go mbeadh socal choíche
Ag a té bheadh ann
'Séard a dúirt Josie Burca, Go mba gheall le dúiche
Bhí ag Tom 's ag Seán, Ó Dhuíche Chlemant
Go drain a Mháillaigh 'S nar bhréa an rása
A bhíodh ag Mula Tom
'S é Pat Mhike Sheáinín a rinne an t-amhrán
'S ní bhfuair sé morán ach áit don laoí
Dúirt Ghallagher dá mbeadh sé posta

Go bhfaigheadh sé gabhaltas amuigh thuas i Meath

Anois nach bhfuil sé 's gan súil go deo leis

Tá trua mhór ann do na gcomharsanaí

A fuair droch thalamh 's fraoch doite 's

Beidh an ráta an mhór orthu i gcaitheamh a tsaoil

'Séard a dúirt Mamaí Walsh nach talamhaí an Gréasaí

Nó éinne eile a bhfuil ag an snámh

Ach a piocadh míoltóg ó thús an tséasúr

'S ag gcrochadh leofa amach sa bhád

Siad na Terrys óga a bhéas go gloite a rithe leofa anon 's anall

Leagan Pat Mhike Sheán agus Máirtín Terry

Stripping of Kilbride (translation)

'Yes', said Mammy Walsh, let it be said

'And the townlands are made' That will be the word forever -
The way it will be

'Yes, Josie Burca said, that was about a townland Tom Seán,
from Clemant's place

Who had that cursed drain and loved to race with Tom 's mule

The song was composed by Pat Mhike Sheáinín 'And he found
little but a place for the calf

Gallagher said if he were married That he would get a holding
out above in Meath

Now it's not that they will be away forever They have great pity
for the neighbours

That had bad land and burnt heather, and rates will be great for them throughout their lives

'Mammy Walsh said the shoemaker is not a landowner nor is anyone else who is swimming about Picking Mayflies from the beginning of the season That they'll have to hang out in the boat

Extra bit written by Pat Mhike John and Martin Terry

They are the young Terrys who will have glory running with them back and forth

I personally did not bother with the latest fashions; I was happy that I had on a new suit and was delighted to listen to traditional music with a beer in my hand. I loved to have the craic with everyone up at the bar, to hear how everyone was doing and if I got half a chance, to play the box. Petie Welsh and John Coyne, both terrific box players, entertained us for hours with a rich traditional sound as a young Marcus Philbin would start to sing. Even though I saw the changes happening around me, I felt at home. Back in England when I wasn't listening to traditional music, I discovered an up-and-coming country singer, Seamus Moore, whose songs were mighty altogether. Any man or woman who left Ireland to work on building sites in England understood these songs; they weren't sad and mournful like so many other Irish country songs, they were funny and realistic, sometimes too realistic! Seamus' music was a tonic to listen to and great craic.

That Christmas Eve, I was introduced to Mary Philbin. I knew Mary was a sister of Jimmy and Marcus who were great musicians. She was also the girl who, because of my sister, was left totally stew less from Tuesdays onwards.

As usual, I was propping up the bar with the lads, putting the world to rights when Mary started to chat to me; she didn't hold back about the loss of her stews. She was great craic and very chatty, telling me that she was working temporarily in Galway in an office. She had great plans to escape to the bright lights of London, complaining that her only visitor all week was her younger brother Michael, an exceptional Irish dancer who travelled to stay with her overnight and attend classes. Galway was a stopgap, she excitedly told me, explaining that she was coming to England to go nursing after Christmas. Mary clapped loudly, with great enthusiasm, as Marcus finished playing, she was justifiably proud of both of her brothers' music and clearly loved having young Michael visit so she could spend time with him and treat him in the local café every week. In that meeting I felt I knew so much about Mary; she had an infectious laugh and a mischievous glint in her brown eyes that had me totally captivated. She had a total devil-may-care attitude as she tossed her long red hair over her shoulders and laughingly explained that she had failed some entrance exams in nursing in Lancashire but hadn't let that stop her. "I did them again and got into Ashford to start in February!" She laughingly proclaimed.

It was her attitude that enthralled me; she was fiercely protective of her brothers, family oriented, could obviously cook brilliantly and was stubbornly determined. I knew she was Tommy Welsh's first cousin and tried to glean more information from Tommy who just mumbled something about her being a nice girl.

I couldn't get Mary Philbin out of my mind that Christmas. Her directness was so refreshing, she was not trying to be anybody else other than who she was, she was full of life and sometimes outrageous. I knew I needed to see her again. On St Stephen's night I caught a glimpse of Mary in 'The Larches' with her friends, so I made sure I managed to chat to her to ask if she was going to the dance in Cong after the pub. She gave me a laugh and said, 'Where else would I be going?' I decided I'd see her there and that was where the trouble began. Tommy and the lads were in fine form and were in no hurry to leave 'The Larches' that night to go dancing in Cong, even though we had discussed it earlier. John Coyne was giving us all Christmas drinks, the drink was flowing, and the music was great, the story telling began and each man settled down for the night to outdo each other talking about shafts dug, shoring put up and digging holes. I usually enjoyed this craic, but that night I was in no mood; I was on edge as the night wore on. Midnight came and went; one o'clock came and still nobody made a move. Eventually, as I was the only one with a car, they decided to move. I had to make two runs of it that night as so many people had decided last minute to go to the dance in Cong. My good deed backfired as I didn't get to the dance until twenty-five past one, just as the national anthem began. I spied Mary across the hall and walked up to her quickly, 'I thought you were never coming,' she grinned as she held my eye, turned, walked off and said, 'Goodnight'.

I had just enough time to arrange to meet her in 'The Larches' the following night. We met up and hit it off straight away. I knew Mary was going over to stay with her aunt Ann Fahy, and to start her nurse's training, so I made sure I got Ann Fahy's number.

Mary and I saw each other a lot after she came to England. She loved it in London and found everything exciting, even down to the orange streetlights! We went dancing, like most of our generation in London and we went to Irish pubs such as 'The Orange Tree', 'The Swan' in Stockwell, 'The Cricketer' in Kennington, 'The Crown' in Willesden and 'The Foresters' in Tooting, always with Mary's brother Tommy who was living in London, and sometimes with Liam Mulroe and Tommy Walsh.

Elizabeth McAndrew continued to help us learn about food, Mary was introduced to them and of course also to the fine dining. We would grin at each other across the linen-clad table as we stared at more cutlery before us than either of us had seen in any drawer back at home. McAndrew fell under Mary's charm; she was then nursing in Ashford, having completed her training and I enjoyed listening to them chat together. Mary could talk to anyone and there were no awkward silences around any table with Mary present. The topic of conversation would veer from sport, both soccer and GAA, to politics, from family at home to opportunities in London. Mary was a great conversationalist and I got to know the McAndrews even more as they opened up to her. I had decided to buy the third machine the Christmas after I met Mary, and it was a good decision. It was paying off. Soon I was in a position to buy a fourth machine without a loan and did so, but I still needed to get the work. In 1972 when I bought my first machine, I had started my own company and because of McAndrew's involvement called it Flannery Plant Hire (Oval) Ltd. Back then it was just me and my only machine and it didn't really feel like a company, but now with the prospect of the fourth machine, the company felt much more like a proper business.

Weekends were spent wherever the best music was to be heard. We enjoyed traditional music sessions and also the country and western scene where big bands would headline in the 'Galtymore' or the 'Galty' as we called it. It seemed everybody in London ended up in the 'Galty' each weekend. It was like home from home having the craic with Peadar Frank and Maureen, Mairtín Sonny, Liam Mulroe and Cathy, Patrick and Tommy Philbin. It was dear enough to get in, especially for a couple, so I remember offering a doorman cash in hand to let us in for half price. We soon had a regular little arrangement. Mary loved to go to the 'Galty' when she was off work just as much as I did. It was no longer a place where I had to do the walk of shame across the floor. I had Mary by my side and the world was a better place. It was in the 'Galty' we would meet friends, dance the night away and have fun. They were carefree happy days. I was working hard; Mary was nursing and the Irish scene at the weekends was our release; time to enjoy each other's company.

After three and a half years we decided to get married. There was no big romantic proposal. I don't remember planning to ask the question; we just knew. Nowadays there is so much hype around getting married and proposing that it seems incredible that we just went shopping and bought a black sapphire engagement ring, chosen by Mary. To us it was romantic and exciting enough, and we were dying to share our good news. My sister Barbara, over for the summer working in Lloyd's bank, was one of the first people we told. Mary wrote to our parents to let them know. Both sets of parents knew each other very well and wrote back to say they were delighted with our news.

I found it financially difficult enough at that stage with my mortgage in Tottenham; the repayments of my loans for my increasing number of machines, coupled with the fact that Mary and I had set a date to get married and we needed to find a home. I remember being aware for the first time that I really had a lot on my plate.

McAndrew and I had worked together regularly, and I now had four machines as well as two hymacs. They were a problem to maintain, however I did have lots of hire from Wimpey. The biggest issue I had was getting drivers to work my machines as my plant was only as good as the drivers I had to work it. This caused me no end of trouble; drivers would commit to doing a job and then not turn up. I have many memories of finishing up one job and rushing to fix machines on another site in the evenings. I was concerned and fully aware that any poor production on my part or on my drivers' part would have a negative impact on my growing reputation within Wimpey.

We also had another issue to contend with; we had to decide where to live. Mary was keen to live near her aunt in Kenton however we couldn't afford to buy a house there unless I sold my house in Tottenham. In 1975 that is what I ended up doing.

Mary helped me choose the house in Holland Road. The house was what we would refer to nowadays as a project. In other words it was a bit of a wreck and needed lots of work done to it. We didn't care about that of course; we saw no problems at all and were delighted that this was going to be our new home. It was a really exciting time in our lives, Mary's brother Francis, who was a great craftsman, came over to help me when I moved into the house.

I wonder now, when I look back, what spurred me on at that time. I feel that I was beginning to be a little nervous about what I was doing and how my loans were mounting up. It may have been because I was getting married and the hope of starting a family made me a little more cautious than I had been previously. I really don't know. But with Mary's infectious enthusiasm and her obvious delight at the idea of her new house in Wembley, I pushed those thoughts to the back of my mind.

I had more to focus on as Mary and I started to plan our wedding for July 31st, 1976. In truth as with most Irish men I knew, I had very little to do with it other than going up to Paddington to shop in 'High and Mighty' to buy my suit the Saturday before we went home. Mary had organised everything else. I felt great to have a suit that fitted me well. We didn't go to any great expense; we didn't have the money to spare. Every penny I made went straight back into the business.

Mary and her cousin Kathleen Welsh went shopping and bought her dress in Harlesden, along with three bridesmaid's dresses. Mary was buying her dresses out of her nurse's salary and didn't want to spend too much. She was thrilled with her purchases, but I remember Mary telling me that she knew her mother was disappointed when she saw her dress because she thought the neck was too high, and it was too modest. Nevertheless, Mary loved the style of the dress and wasn't too bothered.

I had never seen Mary wear make up until that day. She looked like a Celtic princess as she walked up the aisle in Cornamona, sunlight catching her auburn hair creating a halo effect that stays with me to this day. As Fr Waldron began the service, I gazed at her. I was the proudest man in the world. Fr Waldron had cast doubt on the whole ceremony earlier in the week when he asked us for our letters of freedom. I think he knew by our blank looks that he had to act quickly. I'll never know how it was resolved, but thankfully the marriage went ahead.

Mary's parents were so proud of their only daughter and wanted her wedding day to be memorable. They paid for the wedding, and nothing was left to chance. Mary's mother employed the Sisters of Mercy to bake the traditional wedding cake and got Stephen Kyne's much sought-after band in the area, who played every genre of music magnificently and encouraged us to dance into the small hours with friends and family in Flannery's hotel in Galway. We had a great day with our friends and family. Many of Mary's nursing friends from England had never been at an Irish wedding and thought I owned Flannery's hotel! McAndrew and Elizabeth travelled over too, although the ceidhlidh music and country sounds were not to their taste and I seem to remember them spending a lot of time sitting in the foyer drinking wine.

As we set off after the wedding for our honeymoon in Kerry, I knew that no matter what life threw at us, we would be stronger together and I also knew with certainty that life with my beautiful wife at my side was never going to be dull. We hadn't booked any accommodation for our honeymoon and stayed our first night in White's Hotel in Ennis. Mary's face, when we sat down to breakfast only to notice the Burke sisters from Cornamona cast knowing glances at us, is a memory that will last me a lifetime. I couldn't stop laughing but Mary was mortified knowing that they knew we had spent our first night together!

Chapter 7
Trouble and Strife

Mary and I settled into married life in Holland Road. We were so happy in our lovely, three bed semi-detached house in a typical tree lined London suburban road. We even had a park at the end of the cul-de-sac that added that little extra bit of greenery and openness to the area. Mary's brother Francis and I had worked hard fixing up the house. We had rewired, replastered and replumbed it and put in central heating. We were delighted with ourselves; we were really proud owners.

Mary had decided to leave Ashford and was working as an agency nurse in Holloway prison. She had an interview process that was a true sign of the times we were living in when they asked her about the IRA. We were in no way political at all, and I remember how surprised Mary was to be asked questions about her politics which would never be allowed today, but that was the way it was. Mary worked there on a part-time basis for a while and then was offered a full-time staff nurse position. But we had decided we wanted to start a family as soon as possible.

Now the wedding was over, and we were back in Wembley, my mind had fixated once again on my growing JCB and Hymac fleet. I continued to have serious issues getting reliable drivers. It wasn't the cost of my growing fleet or the repayment of loans that kept me awake at night but the worry of whether a driver would actually turn up to do his shift. I remember one driver was so unreliable that every morning, I used to have to travel from Wembley to his house in Hayes; a distance of only thirteen miles but in rush hour could take up to forty minutes and throw stones up at his window to wake him up to make sure he arrived on site. It was ridiculous really, but he just wouldn't get up if I didn't go and wake him. That man broke my heart and my spirit. He was a good driver, but I wondered if it was worth the torment to get him to work. I remember the annoyance of it all very clearly, cold frosty mornings when I had my own driving job to do and having to drive out of my way for him made me feel very annoyed and wonder, not for the first time, if it was all worth it at all. Not only was he making me look bad because he was late on site, but he was making me late too. Luckily the foreman I was working with knew me from previous jobs. He gave me some leeway when I told him my problem, he understood my issues. I did this for a couple of months, determined to make a success out of this devil of a driver when all of a sudden, he decided driving wasn't for him. He told me that it was not the life for him being woken up so early to go and drive each day. I was speechless, but what could I do? It was his life, and I could do nothing and so said nothing. To give him his due, he introduced me to another driver, Noel Kearns from County Offaly, who unlike himself, was determined, efficient, professional in his approach and most importantly of all, a great timekeeper. Noel got me out of a lot of trouble.

At that time, I was really uncertain about what I was doing, I hated relying on people to turn up for work. It really annoyed me that there were people who were like that. They couldn't be depended on at all, but I was in too deep to do anything about it. I really wanted to make it work out, but I must admit when I could see other fellas from home working hard and enjoying themselves at the weekend without a care in the world, I was a bit jealous of their carefree lives. I seemed to have the weight of the word on my shoulders, having sleepless nights worrying about people turning up for their shift the next day. They, on the other hand, worked hard for the money in their pocket, work was plentiful, and they didn't have the constant worry of loan repayments and drivers. Such things had begun to be all I thought about. It was a worrying time for me without doubt.

Meanwhile, Mary and I were delighted that she was now pregnant with Martin. We were so excited at the idea of having a baby. During her pregnancy Mary had found a job in a place near our home and she was very busy making our house a home. She didn't want to continue nursing when Martin was born, and we agreed that it would be great for the business if she worked from home and looked after bookings for the fleet of six machines. There were always issues that I couldn't deal with as I was out driving myself, so I needed Mary to be the point of contact with clients. I suppose we both underestimated the amount of time needed to look after a baby. It was a hard time. Mary was the backbone of the operation. She had to work really hard behind the scenes. Mary had a great way with her.

She put clients at ease if there were any little issues. Her straight-talking manner made sure we got hire for my machines and her determined attitude meant that we got paid. Mary would have no qualms telling contractors that a machine was on the way and would be with them shortly even though she knew I was out on another job desperately trying to fix a problem to get a machine going. I was the mechanic as well as the driver. The main issue we had really was that because there were no mobile phones; we had no way of contacting each other than when I phoned home from a phone box for an update on how things were going at home. This was terrible for Mary because often she had no idea where I was or what I was doing but she would have to pretend she knew and hope I got back in touch from the payphone.

Mary would have to fend off irate contractors wondering when a machine was going to turn up or when a machine was going to be fixed, all the while wishing I would phone in and let her know what was going on. She had to be quick witted, wily and astute. There was no doubt about the stress this caused. Mary had a young baby to look after, a new house, as well as helping me to grow the business. She put her heart and soul in it and was behind me all the way. Mary didn't attend and was not interested in attending mother and baby lessons, or so she had me believe. She maintained that she had to be at home in case we would miss a hire. I could never have managed without her really, even though it was not something I ever voiced or expected of her. I definitely knew however, that I had a soulmate who would be by my side no matter what.

I was able to put my mind on the work on site because I knew Mary had things under control at home. I didn't have to worry about paying bills or chasing work and I knew that she would do everything in her power to keep things going.

Mary had a great pride in our house. It was so homely and tidy; I loved to return home every evening to the smell of baked apple pies and a steaming hot dinner. I look back now and don't know how she did it, how either of us did it. Mary's love of fun and socialising meant that we soon had lots of friends in Holland Road. People were constantly popping in for a chat, which is just as well for I was seldom there.

Two years and two months after Martin was born, our second child, Patrick arrived, and I could see that Mary was getting a little restless. She was so good at multi-tasking but her desire to nurse never left her. Mary had worked so hard to get that qualification. Her education at the technical school in Cornamona ended at sixteen, as it did for every child attending that school at that time. The purpose of the school was to provide every pupil with a vocational qualification and Mary had learned book- keeping and secretarial skills; great skills indeed, except Mary wanted to do nursing. Her great friend Liam Mulroe remembers Mary as being very clever at school and standing out from the crowd. No matter how clever she was, Mary struggled to get a training position for nursing in Ireland because she had not completed her Leaving Certificate, but she was determined. During the Mayfly season at home, Mary used to work in a little bed and breakfast, and she had come across Bernie Murphy, a doctor who frequented Tourmakeady for the fishing. They got chatting and he promised to put in a recommendation for her to get a place in a training hospital in England. She travelled to Lancashire where she applied unsuccessfully to train. Mary was more than a little put out when the nuns in Lancashire quipped,

"Oh, I see Barney still likes the red heads!"

Mary's feeling of belittlement at the hands of those nuns in a strange way made her all the more determined to succeed, which of course she did shortly afterwards in Ashford, Surrey.

It had not been an easy journey for Mary, and I knew she felt she was wasting the nursing training she had received. She knew that her parents had been really proud when she had graduated and she wanted to be successful in her own right, not just to be seen as an administrator for me. Her parents had only one daughter and had made sacrifices for her to travel to England to train as a nurse. I could see that it meant a lot to her and although I really needed her to help, I couldn't justify standing in her way when I was following my own dreams.

Mary had seen a post in the newly opened Clementine Churchill Hospital in Sudbury Hill, and decided that was where she wanted to be. The shift pattern she began there meant that she could be at home to look after the boys until I returned in the evening. She was very enthusiastic that she could make it work. Mary also confided in me that her further ambition was to complete further training and become a health visitor. I knew how ambitious she was. Indeed, that was one of the many qualities I had admired about her when we first met, but I was worried that I would not be able to fulfil my commitment to the boys to be home in the evening. Increasingly, I had problems with machines breaking down, drivers not turning up and people not paying for work done. I hadn't exactly been a hands-on father at that stage. I was always either at work or chasing work and found it difficult to see how I could change things. I was a bit concerned.

We argued about it; I knew Mary felt that my ambition was costing her a lot and my involvement with the children wasn't as much as either of us wanted it to be. I was worried about her working late shifts, worried that I wouldn't make it home to look after the children and even if I managed that, would I have had enough time to get my machines ready for hire? I knew I would have to do what I could to make it work.

One man I met in Holland Road and who became a lifelong friend was John O'Brien. He and his wife Bridie lived across the road from us, and I had seen him around when Francis and I were doing the house up. John, from Bansha, Co. Tipperary was a tall lean and dark-haired man. Full of chat and purpose; I had seen him leave for work early like myself and knew he worked in construction. He had made several attempts to come over and chat when we were doing up the house, but I didn't really engage him in conversation. I don't really know why; it just wasn't in my nature to make small talk, and I was keen to get on with it and complete the refurbishment work on the house before I could move in. John was an inquisitive character, and it was clear he wanted to be friendly, but I had little to say to him. However, now Mary was around, things soon changed.

Mary, being as talkative as John, found a friend, and so John and his Kerry wife, Bridie, became like family. They used to laugh at how reluctant I was initially to make conversation, but they never held it against me as they introduced us to their social scene at the club up in St Joseph's, Wembley, where they loved waltzing, jiving and having fun. John had worked as a bouncer at the Galtymore so he knew everyone. John and Bridie were good for us; they introduced us to lots of people and to Ivy, who became our regular babysitter, and so, we could go out and enjoy our Saturday nights. With John and Bridie, we soon became regulars down at the club.

It was a great social scene for us as a young married couple. Liam Mulroe and his wife Cathy were in Willesden and Mairtín Coyne and Barbara lived in Hayes, so we had plenty of friends to go out with and we all met up often. It was great to have friends from home. I remember that time as being great craic, but things don't stay the same for long. Lots of people went back home when their children came along and were ready to start school. We were sad when our friends decided to move back but that was the way of life back then, not everyone wanted to stay.

In Holland Road, we lived in a lovely tightknit community, where people were keen to help each other out. I remember lending Mary's car to John on many an occasion when his own didn't start. It would be gone when Mary woke up and she'd go mad because she then had to walk the children to school. I could see her point, but I couldn't see a neighbour stuck. Everybody in that street was working hard trying to make a living. John and Bridie owned their own construction company, J&B Construction and John became somebody I could talk to. In him I found somebody I could trust. Like all Irish people living away from home, we kept up some of the old traditions we used to enjoy, especially when it came to food, drink and celebrations.

John used to go to the bakery in Alperton every Saturday morning and return home with delicious soda breads, Irish butter and all manner of sweet stuff. When he had the tea ready, he would call us over to his house and we would spend the morning around his kitchen table having the craic. He was a great storyteller and would have us in stitches with stories of his work in Bromley, most of the stories totally exaggerated and we knew it but didn't care at all. Later on, their children, Carmel,

Tony, Johnny and Paul became our regular babysitters. Carmel even came back to Kilbride to help Mary out during the long school holidays, although herself and my sister Bridie became such good friends that not much babysitting was done. Tony and Paul used to love to help me tinker with machine parts in the garage at weekends. John and Bridie were salt of the earth people, we loved their company.

Another chance meeting that led to a lifelong business relationship and friendship was the day Mary met Ian Keysner. We had realised our insurance brokers in Sudbury were not providing us with a good enough deal. We had eight machines in 1979 and the cost of insuring them against theft was growing. We were being charged far too much. Armed with the yellow pages, Mary went on the hunt for somebody who we could work alongside. She saw Hibernian Insurance and the Irish name was the main reason we met our new insurance broker.

This is where I really appreciated her grit and determination. I didn't have a minute to spare but we had to do something and needed to get a better deal, so Mary decided she would go and sort it out. She walked into the insurance broker in Alperton and met Ian.

Ian, son of an Austrian father and London born mother, had recently started out on his own and had taken over a brokerage called Hibernian. He later told us himself that he didn't have a clue that Ireland in Latin was Hibernia but was pleasantly surprised when so many Irish businesses approached him attracted by the name. He had worked hard to set up his business and had struggled to achieve the five-thousand-pound loan he needed to establish himself. A solicitor friend of his, Joe Bateman, introduced him to a bank manager of the Bank of Ireland in Shepherds Bush where he was successful in getting the loan to start his business. He received the offer letter with a sentence ending

"Remember who helped you out when you needed it."

And so, began a lifelong association with the Irish businesspeople and Irish businesses. Ian was determined to get the best rates he could and so it was equally good for us when Mary walked into the office, tired, and frazzled with baby Martin running around making a total nuisance of himself. Never one to be put off by something like a small child causing havoc, Mary began to discuss what she expected and needed from an insurance broker.

Mary was so strong; she had recently heard reports of our competitors sneering at her for trying to run a family and a business. They looked down their noses at us, telling anyone who would listen that Flannery's could not be taken seriously as the wife conducted business with one child on her hip and the others bawling at her feet whenever she answered the phone or met clients. Mary was privately upset that people were mocking her for trying her best to make a living, but in public, she made sure nobody knew how that comment had hurt her. She portrayed a very different figure, full of confidence as she pretended to laugh at these comments and carried on.

Mary's mispronunciation of the word "excavator" had been corrected by a receptionist. Mary had mistakenly requested an "escavator" instead and had been mimicked on the phone for not knowing what she wanted. Mary simply laughed this nastiness off, showing a real strength that would be crucial in developing our business in future years. However, while she laughed these things off, she never forgot them.

This strength of character became evident when Mary met Ian. Mary approached Ian in his office with two with screaming toddlers in tow. Whatever Ian thought, Mary was not put off when he decided it was in his best interests to meet in calmer surroundings. He agreed to meet us at home at Holland Road. Ian would later admit that he liked us immediately. He too came from humble beginnings and explained that he had a gut feeling about working with us. He saw us as honest, decent people with integrity and so began a lifelong friendship as well as a business acquaintance.

Ian helped me take on the banks at one stage when I was badly advised on a huge commercial loan, resulting in me taking out an absurd amount of insurance that was akin to blackmail. The banks made an impressive case, but we won, and I received compensation. Ian wanted me to take it further, but I was satisfied with what I received. I didn't need any more and had made my point.

"De réir a chéile a thógtar na caisleáin" – bit by bit we build the castles. (Irish proverb)

I admit to chasing a good deal but don't consider myself a greedy man. Ian was, and still is, a great financial adviser to our family. He is more risk averse than me, but the relationship worked. Ian jokes that he is glad I didn't always listen when I took on the risky investments. He says this because most of them were fruitful.

It was Ian who later suggested that we move from Holland Road to a bigger house a little further out of town. He himself had done so and never regretted it for one minute. We were much too busy to even consider moving when he initially suggested it. We loved living in Holland Road. but eventually we heeded Ian's advice.

It soon became clear that we needed to get some help with the administration. Mary had to give up her job at the Clementine Churchill hospital, because we just couldn't make it work. As I was concerned would happen, I was never at home to look after the boys, and we were constantly relying on our neighbour Ivy to make things work out. Financially it made no sense. When our third child Maria arrived, Mary was incredibly busy at home.

John O'Brien used to come over to visit us when we were doing our invoices. He made himself at home, heating up Mary's home-made apple pies while smoking profusely over our shoulders as he waited for us to finish. Sometimes we worked into the small hours. It was relentless. We had so many jobs to cover and while Mary was great keeping tabs on our invoices, it was at a heavy cost to family life.

To keep in touch with family, Mary went home for every summer holiday. She was very close to her mother and brothers and every summer was filled with joy and happiness. We had built our home in Kilbride in 1986 so stayed in our own house, which was beside my parents' home. The children played outside in the fields and visited Mary's family in Cornamona daily. When I went home, we made sure to take both sets of parents out to 'The Larches' most nights. I remember when I was going out with Mary everyone in Cornamona seemed to jump into the back of the car for the lift to 'The Larches' and so it was just the same after we were married. We often had Michael, Marcus, the parents and even our neighbour Mike Comiskey used to hop in as I made my way, car full, all laughing and joking around the lake to the pub.

These were hair raising drives, the roads were narrow, winding and high. I remember Billy Murphy had an automatic white Hillman Minx convertible home one summer, and when everybody piled inside, I decided to drive. I was keen to see how it would handle the roads back home. I could hardly take the bend it was so full of people and bottles of beer. Only for Liam Mulroe bending over to dislodge a bottle from behind the pedal as I was driving, we would have all landed in the lake. Liam was a bit rattled by this experience and I remember him shouting at me,

"Paddy, if a bomb went off beside you, you'd stay calm and carry on!"

The summers were special to me. I used to bring bully beef home for the younger ones, Nora, Michael and Bridie and they loved it. Bridie hated me calling her Bridilee, but Bridilee she was whether she liked it or not. I felt it was very important to stay connected, I knew well that for them, us older siblings were not seen as part of their childhood growing up. I made sure I wasn't forgotten!

To help us enjoy these long summer holidays, McAndrew took over the invoicing each summer. It was a good deal for us both, but he was getting older and wanted to retire. I suppose it was inevitable really that he would decide the time had come to part company. There is no doubt that I could not have achieved what I had without his help to start me off, but things were different. I now acquired more machines myself and sourced all the hire myself. As Mary and I poured over our takings and invoices, we could see it was probably a good time for us to part ways with McAndrew.

With three children and Mary's time being increasingly taken up with school runs as well as numerous trips to Mayo and Galway, we decided to get an administrator.

For my part I hardly ever saw my children. I was away working when they awoke and didn't return until long after they had gone to bed. It is a wonder they had any idea who I was at all. We knew we couldn't do much about my working hours so decided that Mary needed less stress from the business to raise our growing family. I had come home one evening to see Mary in tears of frustration. Martin used to attempt to and sometimes succeeded in answering the phone, which of course made us look inefficient and unprofessional. Mary's response was to tie up the old dial phone in a plastic bag and knot it so Martin couldn't get to it, however that meant of course that Mary had to untie the bag before she could answer herself and she wasn't quick enough to be successful. She was even worried about missing business during the time she was out doing the school run. We knew we had to do something about this so together we turned our small spare room into a cosy office, hoping we would be able to hire somebody smart enough to learn our business and work alongside us.

At first, we employed a young man to prepare our invoices and VAT returns, however, our inexperience with having an employee and his inexperience in dealing with a business such as ours soon caused us to part ways. We were very disappointed that it didn't work out. The business was growing fast, in 1982 I had 12 machines, and I was fortunate at this time to have some terrific drivers.

I remember one in particular called Joe Staunton. I had gone out to buy a new machine and Joe happened to be driving the one I was purchasing. I could tell from talking to him that he was passionate about his machine and his job. We understood each other well. Joe was from Ballivarry in Co. Mayo and probably because of our similar backgrounds and work ethic, we formed a bond over our machines and Joe decided that if I was going to buy that machine, I would have to take him too. This was a deal I was delighted with. I formed a strong bond of friendship with Joe as well as a long working relationship that lasted until he retired. People like Joe were a pleasure to work with. His passion in life was his machine without a doubt.

Try as I might, I could never get rid of the feeling that no matter how successful I was, everything could disappear overnight. I felt that there was something I wasn't doing quite well enough; trouble was, I didn't really know what it was that I wasn't doing. I knew the home situation with Mary had to improve as I could see she was getting really stressed. I was frustrated that the young lad working from home hadn't worked out and was delighted when John O'Brien told me about a young girl called Caroline Carty who might be suitable for the job.

Chapter 8
The Ladies

I consider that there are many women who played an important part in my life at different times and in different ways. In each of them I can see something of the others. I believe that we are all moulded by the people who went before us; we are moulded by their presence or sometimes by their lack of presence. I'm very proud of my four sisters, Mary, Barbara, Nóra and Bridie. I greatly value their presence in my life. Having our own house at home and visiting every summer had a positive impact on my relationship with them and afterwards, with their families.

I love my two daughters Maria and Julie dearly; they both bring me such happiness. I adore my six granddaughters, Olivia, Isabel, Grace, Molly, Tilly, Edie and Florence while not forgetting of course, my grandsons, Conor, Thomas, Charlie, Arthur and their brother Martin. I am surrounded by strong women, and I am grateful that my sons have found strong women in their wives. However, I want to give thanks to the three women who have exerted a strong influence on me. Women to whom I am indebted whose wisdom, strength and foresight have made a lasting impression.

Julia Joyce, my mother, was the first woman who moulded me into being who I am. Julia was a kind-hearted mother; a quiet woman who left an unforgettable imprint on the lives of each of her children. A tall woman whose strength of character was there for all to see. She had kindly eyes and a gentle soul. She was a woman shaped by circumstance, a woman who made the most out of what was presented to her, a woman who never complained, who looked for opportunity and who did so with humour and grace. Julia Joyce was a brave woman who did not expect much of others but had very high expectations of herself.

As a child, Julia often had to walk miles to school. Most days she arrived wet, barefoot, without the sod of turf she was supposed to bring with her which was needed to keep the fire going. Indeed, on many days, she didn't arrive at all. The nuns in her school were kind to her and did what they could to help her. For their kindness and understanding, Julia was forever grateful.

When Julia married Mairtín Flannery, or Mairtín Terry as he was known. She moved into the whitewashed thatched cottage he shared with his father and accepted that, to make a living, he had to leave to go to England. She played her part well, working on the farm with her father-in-law and making the house homely.

As her eight children entered into this world, Julia gave them love and made a happy home. She was used to making the best of every situation. If she, as a young woman, ever felt resentful that the man she married wasn't around, and her partner in everyday household and farming chores was in fact her father-in-law, I never once heard her complain or even mention it. It was simply the way things were.

Julia was a real people person; she loved to talk. If anyone asked her a simple question, her way of retelling the facts and attention to detail would make sure her answer was never short and ended up as a whole story. Our house was a house where neighbours would visit for hours to play music, sing, dance and chat. My grandfather, who we called Daidí Mór, and who lived with us until he died in 1973, was like a father to us. He was particularly fond of me as I was his namesake. We called Julia, Mamaí. She was a terrific worker, a great homemaker and a woman who also did a lot of the outside work. She made curtains, sewed clothes, mended sheets, grew all her own vegetables and made sure we never had to buy much. Everybody in the family had a job to do, depending on the time of year. In Spring we would sow potatoes for ourselves and the pigs we harvested them in Autumn. We made sure to separate them into pig's potatoes and our own potatoes as we put them into a pit that Julia had dug to keep them fresh. Julia kept pigs and cows; however, our farm was too small for sheep. I think it is interesting that when father suggested moving to a bigger place with the land commission offer, Julia was horrified and sided with grandfather to make sure we would stay where we were. Julia was content; she had made her home and didn't want to be uprooted.

Julia instilled in all of us a strong work ethic; the need to save, and to be frugal. She would scrimp and save, cut buttons off shirts too worn to be useful, save laces out of shoes that had seen better days, and in later years berate us for using too many sheets of toilet roll.

Despite being so frugal, Julia was never mean spirited. Her sister's children visited every summer from England and sometimes they brought friends with them to stay for six weeks. Julia's family homeplace was given to her brother Matty but after he had moved to Meath, the little house that was left on the land was not fit for habitation. It is a testament to the very good relationship my mother and grandfather had that the Joyce nieces and nephews were welcomed with open arms into the Flannery home. Not only were they welcomed but they were given the beds and her own children had to sleep on the floor. Cornflakes and shop bread were bought as Julia fussed that these English children must have shop bought breakfast and would not be used to eating our breakfast and our country ways. Little did she realise then that our organic staple diet was much healthier than any other diet and would be sought after in years to come. These cousins from London and Birmingham, as well as the friends they brought, were very well looked after. We enjoyed their company and remained close friends with them throughout our lives. Julia was settled and very happy in Kilbride; she worked very hard and probably felt a security that had been sadly lacking in her earlier life.

My father Mairtín travelled to England in October and sometimes did not come back until March; Julia never complained. She didn't appear lonely, but I do know that when my father was at home the house was filled with joy and laughter.

My greatest memory of my mother is her work ethic. She was great with the animals and great with the people. Neighbours came for her when they were sick. They came for her to lay out the dead. She visited the old and infirm. It annoyed her in later years when people had cars and drove past her house without calling. She missed the people going over the road who called for a chat and maybe even a few accordion sessions. She missed the sean nós dancing and the way people would gather when they heard "Mrs McCloud's" floating on the breeze meant the house was never lonely. Julia blamed the cars for the fact people got to town and back without the need to stop off for a bit of craic.

My mother's "me" time was on Sunday when she would dress up for Second Mass and go to Clonbur alone while the children would go to First Mass in Finney. It is the only time I ever remember her having any time to herself. Whether she relished this down time as time away from the family to think, to dream, to plan, or whether it was time to simply fulfil her Mass obligations I'll never know. I like to think that during these short-lived moments, as she cycled into Clonbur in her Sunday best, that she was happily planning for the future; a bright one for her and for her family. She made a routine of meeting Mrs Gill and Mrs Welsh as well as Marie Halloran in the shop after Mass and enjoyed catching up with what was going on in her friend's lives.

Julia realised that education was the key to a better life, and I believe that this is what she craved for each of her children. My sister Mary was sent to boarding school which was very unusual at the time. Most girls who boarded were from wealthier families than ours, however it is a credit to my parents' ambition that they paid for Mary to board the year before free education came in. They could see Mary was clever and despite a poor primary education, she had caught up with her peers quickly. Mary had been travelling to secondary school by bus for a year, so travel had to be paid for as well as her education. When education became free the money was used to pay for her boarding to give her an even better opportunity. Barbara was also offered to board but she was perfectly happy travelling with her friends on the bus to school so stayed at home. The younger three also travelled to secondary school with everyone else when free education came in.

Julia certainly commanded my greatest respect; she knew what she wanted and drove herself hard to make sure that she succeeded. The new house was built and improved when finances allowed; she made sure her children were educated, and even though my dyslexia was not understood, it didn't mean she wasn't ambitious for me and that was why she loaned me the money she had so preciously saved, to buy my first grey tractor. She could see that my ambition would take me in a different direction. She had faith in me.

Life should have become much easier for both of my parents when my father stopped working in England. It was sad that my father's eyesight had failed at such a young age and deprived him of the ability to do what he wanted to do around the farm.

Nevertheless, Julia made sure that the house was always ready for the card players, the singers and the neighbours. There was always plenty of tea and bread and in later years a half barrel of porter would appear although she never took it herself, except perhaps for a Bailey's at Christmas. Julia made life fun and didn't take things too seriously.

The second woman who has had a huge influence on my life is my wife, Mary. Mary Philbin is one of seven children, third youngest and the only girl. She always says that is where she learned very quickly to stand her ground. She spent many long summer evenings playing in goals being pummelled by the football her brothers joyfully shot at her. They showed no mercy.

Mary's family are from Cornamona on the other side of the lake in Co. Galway, where Mary's brother Michael inherited the family home and lives there with his wife Peggy and family. We are regular visitors there.

As was usual back then, the Philbin family were hard working, small-holding farmers and the father, Willie, was like the other men, away working in England. Mary remembers quite clearly crying when being asked to kiss the dark, handsome man who had just turned up one evening and was introduced to her as her father. At the age of nine Mary hadn't a clue who this red-haired man with a black striped shirt was. She had seen that he was well received, everyone was delighted to see him, he was great craic, so eventually she happily accepted his outstretched hands as he said

'Ara Mary, a storeen.' (Mary my little love)

Mary remembers this first meeting clearly.

Mary's mother Sarah had worked in England and had enjoyed her time there immensely. Mary always felt that her mother was a little bit sad to return home as war broke out, probably knowing that her life as a housewife in Cornamona was going to be a lot different to the life she had in England. She knew what lay in store, managing all by herself while her husband lived in England.

There was no game of football too rough for Mary. She would tackle like the best of them and according to her brothers, was good at playing dirty. Mary knew that as an only girl in a house full of boys she had something to prove, so she made sure never to show any weakness.

Sarah was a kind and generous woman who used to love to have people visit her home so she could lay out her table with food and drink to entertain. Her attention to detail meant that she set out her table with two of everything so guests would make sure to have what they wanted without stretching over each other. Any child passing by the house would be called in to get a bar of chocolate and if anybody called unannounced, Michael was sent on his bike to the nearest shop to buy ham, cheese and biscuits. I have lovely memories of my mother in law's hospitality.

I saw this determined streak in Mary time and time again as I relied on her for so much in the early days. Mary was always really interested in my work. Her interest in people really helped. She always wanted to understand what made people tick, how they got to where they were in their lives, where they came from and what dreams they had. Mary loved to chat to people, and I have often seen people become more relaxed in her company. In her I see her mother's kindness, her generosity and hospitality reflected.

Mary had and continues to have an honesty that is refreshing, she is her own person. She makes people feel at ease as she probes, cajoles, laughs and works to help them relax. Mary has had to meet lots of people who were better educated, better placed in society, wealthier, better connected than either of us are considered to be, but I can safely say that I never saw her one bit daunted by anyone. It is as if that determination she had as a young girl, having to prove to her brothers that girls are as good as boys, that she could achieve anything they could, stayed with her and never left her.

I saw it help me enormously earlier in my career, as Mary entertained clients. I always felt happier socially with Mary at my side and relied on her to be the one chatting, laughing and making people feel at home. Mary really understood the value in this, so much so that at one stage when we had no money whatsoever to entertain, I decided we were not going out to meet clients for a planned dinner. Mary was having none of it. We robbed Patrick's christening money and booked a table at a fine restaurant in Denham so I could network with the clients and seal the deal. It worked. I remember it so clearly, coming home in the taxi, laughing at having clinched the deal.

It isn't just to get work that Mary employs the tactic of getting straight to the point. I have seen her interact with waiting staff, teachers, shop assistants and newly made friends down through the years to find out what makes them tick and to get to what really matters.

I remember for instance, a Portuguese shopkeeper pouring his heart out to her about the lack of tourists in his patch of Alvor one Easter holiday; she had only gone in for some groceries but all of a sudden, she was meeting the extended family and hearing their tales of woe. Mary made sure that everyone she knew visited this little shop that holiday.

The only time I have ever seen Mary at a loss for words was when our youngest, Julie, was sent to her head teacher's office for poor behaviour. Julie was only four years old and was being punished by being taken off the playground for three days. Julie was furious and told her head teacher that she didn't care about the punishment because her mother was taking her off school to go to Portugal the following day. The head teacher met with Mary to explain what Julie had said and Mary was embarrassed but couldn't deny that she was sneaking off for a holiday during term time. Mary was secretly amused, perhaps realising that in Julie she had met her match.

Mary has always been there for me. I know when she finally gave up her dream of nursing that she was truly sorry to do so. She had worked so hard to achieve this qualification against all the odds. She knew that she had a talent and passion for nursing, and I really didn't want to take that away from her, but I could also see how invested she was in the company. I really needed her determination, bluntness and spirit to help me; to get people to pay me what they owed. Nobody else cared enough to successfully achieve this and we both knew it. I had put up our house against loans when we were in Holland Road and Mary knew that we had to succeed, or we would lose everything. Mary sacrificed her career to help me grow the business and indeed to keep a roof over our growing family's head.

Mary did this graciously; she was frugal and watched our spending. On paper, Flannery Plant Hire Oval Ltd was growing but we both knew that at any stage in those days we could lose everything, even our home.

The third woman who has been influential in my life, in a professional capacity, is Caroline Carty, now Caroline Brown. Although Caroline does not exert the same influence over me as my mother or my wife, in her own way, Caroline is another female without whose influence, Flannery Plant Hire Oval Ltd would not be what it is today.

Caroline joined Flannery Plant Hire Oval Ltd in June 1984 when she was eighteen years of age.

Caroline too had been a little burned in the employment sector, she had left school and gone on to obtain a business diploma. At Wembley job centre she had answered an advertisement to work for a haulage firm who had actually advertised for 'A Girl Friday'. The company soon went into liquidation and Caroline's first foray into the world of work came to an abrupt end.

Her friends had all managed to get more glamorous jobs in the city and when that job finished, Caroline's hope of working close to home to save travel expenses had been dashed. Our neighbour, John O'Brien had heard of her situation and encouraged her to be more prudent in her job selection explaining that she needed to work for a company where her taxes would be paid and she would be looked after properly. John encouraged her to reply to an advert I had posted. I was worried that I wouldn't be able to attract anyone to work in our box room in Holland Rd, however Caroline was delighted to work close to home, and she happily accepted the job offer.

Caroline was a very quick learner. Mary showed her how to do invoices, and she already knew how to keep books. Caroline settled in very well. She seemed delighted to have a local job and one where she was being used effectively. She never seemed to mind that it was a box room with the noises and interruptions of family life nearby. She was very flexible, picking Martin up from St Joseph's School in Wembley as well as answering our increasingly busy phone, chasing debts and keeping records.

Caroline was a breath of fresh air, brilliant at her job and seemed happy to work for us. She even remained with us when we eventually took Ian Keysner's advice and moved to Mulgrave Rd.

We had gone out to look at a lovely estate called Pebworth in Sudbury and had seen a house for sale. Number six Mulgrave Rd was a large, beautiful, detached property with a secluded garden. We spotted a lady who we later came to know as Mrs Mault working in the front garden.

Mary jumped out to find out more about the house while I stayed in the car. She arrived back unusually fed up to tell me that the house was really beautiful but not only was it above our price range, an offer had already been made.

The vendor, Mrs Mault had mentioned that the people who had made the offer were delaying, messing her about and she decided that if we were interested in the house, she would accept a race to bid.

We won the bid and moved into Mulgrave Rd, heavily in debt and astounded at the amount of our first gas bill in such a huge property. To us, it was a palace, and we couldn't believe we lived there. With Mary's encouragement, lots of our old neighbours came for Stations of the Cross held in our house and in the houses of our neighbours.

We were truly delighted with our move. Caroline now had an office at the back of the garage. But the phones didn't stop ringing after Caroline went home and as I was gone at six every morning, Mary was still working very hard. Although on the outside we were beginning to look very successful, we were still up until the small hours trying to get drivers, chasing payments and in truth, we were mortgaged to the hilt as well.

Having Caroline working for us meant that Mary could fly off to Ireland when the children had school holidays without having to involve McAndrew to do invoices and I could travel over for an odd weekend. As the business was going well, I sold the house I bought in Galway some years earlier when I wanted to invest a bit of cash. I then used the proceeds to build a house at home in Kilbride for our holiday home.

Not long afterwards, we noticed that the occupant of a fine house on Amery Road had passed away so Mary went to chat to the owners to see if we could secure a deal which of course she did.

We sold Mulgrave Road because house prices had gone up and I could see a way for us to have an even better house. But the whole episode saw me go on blood pressure tablets for the first time in my life. I believed that to invest in property was the best thing for me to do, but I had huge debts. These debts, coupled with the fact that Mary announced that we were expecting child number four had a bad effect on my health. So, that Easter we decided we needed a holiday and had our first family holiday to the States. It was a lovely time. Days were spent visiting Disney theme parks and providing our children with experiences that we could never have imagined in our wildest dreams.

The move to Amery Road went ahead, and it meant that Caroline had a purpose-built office in the back garden. I had always been keen to expand my business and become involved in groundworks as I could see huge potential, so I established a new company groundworks company.

I was delighted to have this opportunity, and once again put my house up as collateral for this new enterprise. Initially we were quite successful.

Caroline was getting busier; she was efficient and very clever. She picked up the new business as she went along. She was learning on the job. Mary was now taking a back seat and so we had to hire another assistant. In 1988 I remember Caroline saying to me that after forty machines, she needed help. Caroline was a great organiser in the business, and always made sure she could understand every step that had to be taken. Perhaps because there was no specific training for her in this line of work, she was very careful and thorough in every step she took.

Caroline was aware that at any time, if bills were not paid, we could potentially lose our house. She knew we were constantly working in our overdraft; that we sometimes had to hold back payments or that Mary would go ringing around for payment and receive cheques that would invariably bounce. We were always just one step ahead of the bank.

Caroline was taking on new hire, organising drivers, sorting invoices. I had to become more visible around the office but between us we knew where machines were going and how drivers were employed.

I had a core of good drivers, and while the business was growing fast, the associated headaches of drivers not turning up became a constant issue, the more machines we had. Evenings were spent sorting drivers for the next days' work. On many occasions Caroline worked well past clocking off time as she wanted to make sure we were going to be up and ready for the next day and we didn't lose hire because of lateness or absenteeism. On many occasions, if we couldn't source a driver, I had to do it myself.

I had been fortunate to have steady hire with Wimpey, but in truth, in 1988; I was over-extended, my neck was on the line. The banks were getting worried about me.

While Caroline was the backbone of the company, Mary was my backbone. She supported, guided, helped, encouraged, looked for work, cheekily charmed the debtors and insisted on payment. I never really lost my cool. I kept calm because I knew

I had Mary's backing. I did feel stress of course but outwardly I kept a cool head. I knew I could succeed, and Mary did too.

Níor chaill Fear an Mhisnigh ariamh é. (The man with courage never lost) (Irish proverb)

I relied on Caroline a lot. I made sure she received good wages and when assistants came into the business, I also relied on her to train them. Caroline couldn't believe it when people who she thought of as having more expertise or better qualifications than she did couldn't actually understand the running of the business or see what had to be done. We were becoming more and more successful and eventually acquired our own low loader which meant that we didn't have to rely on others to service or move the machines. I had borrowed heavily to buy an office on Watford Rd and a yard in Northolt to keep my machines. My workforce had increased massively, and I now employed more mechanics and fitters, it also meant that Caroline eventually had a proper office.

I was very happy with Flannery Plant Hire Oval Ltd and the way it was performing; my grounds work company was also going from strength to strength, but I could see that labour remained an issue. I decided to establish my own labour supply to see if that would help matters.

Caroline has been steadfast, hardworking and loyal. She has trained personnel into the Flannery way of working. So much so that I was distraught when Caroline started her own family and had to go on maternity leave. I seriously thought that I could never manage the business without her input. When she returned on a part time basis I was delighted. Caroline is somebody who has been with us from the beginning, through the good times and through some very bad times. She has always shown herself to be reliable, honest and above all, extremely clever. Her input in Flannery's has been invaluable. There have been people who joined us, who considered themselves to be better educated, more important and have resented her position in the company so tried to make life difficult. However, her good nature, cleverness and honesty have always shone through, and this is why I always wanted to have Caroline in the business. Caroline was and is very good at seeing through people; she knows whether to trust or not.

Is treise Dúchas ná Oiliúnt. (Nature is stronger than Education)
(Irish proverb)

I am a lucky man indeed to have been raised by Julia Joyce; to have married Mary Philbin and to have employed Caroline Brown. I can see now how each of them has helped me in different ways and at different times of my life.

Julia, for her faith and belief in me daring to go up against the priest for me when all else would have condemned me to a life of bad luck, to giving me the loan of her hard-earned money to buy my grey tractor.

Mary, for being my partner in life, always at my side, through good times and bad times. For believing in me.

Caroline, for being an honest and loyal worker. Somebody I could trust to do her best always, for the business.

The plant hire business back in the day really was a man's domain. I met many fine men who gave me a leg up over the years and they know who they are. In the background, however, are these fine women, women who shaped and moulded me, women who egged me on, and women who were loyal and trustworthy. I pay tribute to these ladies now and always.

Chapter 9
Decision Making in Harrow Weald

What I am going to recall now is a terrible memory for me but if I am to be true to my story it is a tale I need to tell. Nobody becomes successful and has a lovely clear journey to the top without any ups and downs. This story is indeed about a time when I was down, so down that it seemed that there was no way back. So down that I had to summon all my strength and self-belief to carry on. I had no other choice. I am not going to go into great detail about this time in my life. I don't believe it is necessary or healthy to do so. I never look back or let wrongs fester within me. There is no point in that. I am going to talk about a time in my life when I felt things could easily have come crashing down and think about how I felt, how I recovered and leave it at that. I think that's the most important thing that I can do, explain the need to be resilient.

I clearly remember driving through Harrow Weald and not really focusing on where I was going, I was in a sort of fog really. The sweat was dripping down my brow and my stomach was tight with knots. I couldn't believe it; my worst nightmare had happened. All I had worked so hard for was about to be brought into question and I hadn't seen it coming. I think that was what annoyed me the most. I was like a caged animal and "divil the bit of me" was going to accept it. I felt cornered, betrayed. As I thought about everything, from deep inside I could feel a cool anger taking over. I knew I had to get myself out of this situation somehow.

The spring sun was shining in the morning sky as I left the house. I had to get away to think. I had to be alone. The hedgerows were coming into bloom and the season was nudging the sleepy Harrow fields, or what was left of them, to life. I loved this time of year when everything was beginning to wake up from a long winter. I wished, without doubt, that morning, that I had been satisfied with a different life. Why had I done what I did? I had a good life, I loved Kilbride, I loved going to 'Maire Luke's' and 'The Larches'. I loved being alongside my family and friends. I understood them and they understood me. I enjoyed the craic in London on the building sites so why did I not just leave it there and be done with it? Why did I have to chase more, why did I have to do that? I wondered if it was a conscious choice or was it just me reacting in the only way I knew how.

I thought of my father, how hard he had worked to build us our new home, how my mother had worked so we could all make something of ourselves. Had I taken too many risks? Had I trusted too much? Was I too ambitious? Can you be too ambitious? My mind was a whirlwind. I knew I was in a bad place.

During that drive my mind had drifted back to Kilbride, to happier and simpler times and I allowed myself the joy of looking back, thinking of a different path I could have taken. I thought of how my sister Mary had teased me laughingly when I insisted on calling the calf "Bulleen" and looked after it like a pet. I thought of Marcus up the stack pretending to shout at us for porter. I thought of the hours I would spend out on the lake all alone in the shadows of the surrounding mountains. I thought of home.

I knew of course that it was rose tinted memory. As the old folk were fond of saying 'you can't survive on the view'. All the same the memories of home were fond memories of a bygone life.

The eighties had arrived and brought their fair share of issues. People were leaving Ireland in their droves, but there was a difference, this time the people that emigrated were educated. People might have left rural Ireland in the eighties just as they had done in the sixties and early seventies, but now they were leaving for professional jobs. It was easier to make something of yourself with a bit of education.

In the early nineties, Ireland seemed to be more prosperous. People had a bit of money. Employers had access to a ready and educated workforce at home, Ireland was doing well.

I had chatted with Mary earlier in the week. I didn't know if I could summon the energy to fight the fight I knew was coming, so I had discussed the possibility of returning home just like many of our friends were doing. We had money saved, we had our house, and we had land. We could start again back at home; things were a little bit different back there now, more hopeful.

Mary wasn't for it. She wasn't going anywhere. She knew that we had to fight for what we knew was right. We both knew that. We also knew that going home when things got tough was never going to be the answer. Deep down I admired her conviction, her strength, her courage. I admired her greatly; I knew she was up to it, and we had a long journey ahead. It was all I needed really, to know I had her by my side. I had to give it my best shot. What was happening was wrong and I needed to sort things out.

I felt I was back in Kilbride standing in the classroom; the big fella who was too ambitious. I felt hunted down. I didn't know who to trust. In saying something, in speaking out loud, I was as good as admitting that I didn't have full control of the situation. I really wished I'd paid more heed to that old saying 'I ngan fhios don saol is fearr a bheadh ann' (unknown to the world it is better to be) and had kept my head down. Then nobody would care about Paddy Flannery; nobody would be trying to quietly and stealthily take over and rob me.

I had to stop driving so I pulled into a layby to let the feeling of annoyance pass. I rested my head against the headrest and closed my eyes. I imagined I was back in Kilbride with my friends. In my mind's eye, we were lying on our stomachs holding our sides laughing after spending the afternoon skimming stones. Pádraig was in full flow telling stories after we returned from our daily stalking activities looking for the Mayo Indians. I must have drifted off then because the next thing I knew I heard a banging sound from across the street and men's voices shouting directions. When I looked up, I saw a JCB at work and there, all along the arm of it was the name 'Flannery' in big bold letters across it.

I knew then. I knew I would fight for everything I had built up and what's more, I knew with a grim determination that to get rid of the rot that had set in, I needed to start quickly and speak up. I had to voice my concerns and try to figure out who was with me and who was against me. I didn't really have the appetite for it, but I had no choice. If I didn't get rid of the nest of vipers that had moved in, I would have absolutely nothing left to fight for. I had good people to advise me, but even they were out of their depth.

I have always considered myself to be a shrewd judge of character; I seem to be able to read people fairly quickly and this gut instinct has, for the most part, stood me in good stead. It really annoyed me now that this skill seemed to have deserted me.

I had no need for the trappings of wealth but did have a deep urge to forge on. I wonder if my thinking was as a result of listening to the old folk back home who were hell bent on having land and houses. I wondered also was it that we always hear the voices of our forefathers? Was this a burden or a blessing?

I know I am a risk taker. In the nineties, I had secured a financial position for myself that would ensure a good standard of life for me and my family for the rest of my life, but I was never going to be content with just that, I had to keep going. I remember coming home to Mary one evening after I heard there was a yard for sale in Wembley. We were outgrowing our place in Northolt and to have this yard would mean I could have the offices and machines all in one place. It made sense to me, and I could see no reason why I shouldn't do it. Mary could though. She knew it was going to be difficult to convince the banks to lend us the money but that didn't stop her getting on the phone the next morning to try. She was right. They were not so happy to lend the huge amount we needed, Mary threatened to take our custom elsewhere and so after making sure we took out a very expensive insurance on the loan, we were ready to go. That insurance was outrageous, and I found out a few years later that they should never have asked us to take out that policy at all. I paid through the nose for that loan, but it was worth it.

I was considered courageous and driven by many. I honestly cannot say whether this was the case or whether it was simply self-belief that propelled me forward. I just thought to myself 'Why shouldn't I do that?' Sometimes, I think it was almost a recklessness on my behalf that I just didn't consider the consequences. But I don't know, maybe I just didn't worry about it.

I do know also that this event pushed my self-belief to its very limits. I know I'm very good at maths and not just because of the shilling the teacher gave me back in Kilbride! I could instantly work out the detail in any financial contract. I have found that I have an almost photographic mind when it comes to maths. I never wanted to show off this ability to the world or be boastful, but I could see that I had a talent in this area and learned to trust my instincts.

All of this was going through my mind that morning sitting in my car in Harrow Weald, I considered all the fine people who worked alongside me. People I knew well, people who I employed, people I worked for. Everyone was doing their best. I considered my business; it was a fine business without doubt. I was doing well; I had established some subsidiary companies, and I had enough money made to be relatively well off for the rest of my life even after paying off my loans.

I knew though that things were about to unravel.

The way I built up my business was an organic process; the companies I founded were established to meet a growing need. I like to be self-reliant and didn't want to outsource work if I could start a company and do it myself.

I used the same business model I had when I was sixteen back in Kilbride when I had the old grey tractor. I could do so much with the tractor but when I saved my profit and added the trailer, I could do a bit more. Then, when that was successful, and I added my plough, I could expand even further. I was essentially doing the same thing with my plant hire company but on a larger scale. The only difference was that instead of using some of my profit to buy a Honda 50, I began to invest in property.

I sometimes think that perhaps I had some sort of a premonition; I had no reason to worry about my ventures, but I could sense that something was not right. There was no sense of harmony in the business, no sense of togetherness. I could see a split developing in the people around me. I had employed people to help me to develop my businesses further. I knew for sure that there were issues in the office, but I couldn't really get to the bottom of it. I didn't like it; politics was not something I ever had to deal with.

There was definitely some distrust and sides were being taken. Issues that never bothered anyone before were suddenly everywhere. Complaints and distrust were now an everyday reality. I found myself frequently having to defend staff I really trusted. Some people in the business were ambitious for sure and that was a quality I admired, but I was saddened to realise that for some of them, what they had was never enough. The way things were was a threat, a thorn in their side. They wanted more.

I was still bankrolling my subsidiary companies by putting my house up as collateral; I was still repaying huge loans, so my focus was on getting work, doing work and making a good name for myself. Then, suddenly, things in the office quietened down. There didn't seem to be any tension. Things seemed to be better and I with hindsight I should have looked into this to really understand why. In truth though, I was delighted that the infighting seemed to have stopped, and I was all too eager to carry on as if nothing had happened. The reality though was that things were not as they seemed.

Recession was really beginning to bite; it was a terrible time. Companies were going to the wall daily, houses were being repossessed, the manufacturing industry which had been in decline was utterly spent. The Channel Tunnel project had finished and on completion, many hundreds of miners, labourers, chippies, fitters and every known tradesman that had ever set foot on English soil were on the marketplace. There was a glut of men available and, given the saturation of the labour market, our labour company closing was inevitable.

I went looking for professional advice. I knew I needed help; somebody who had the knowledge to guide me and explain clearly what the issues were. A few phone calls later I found myself sitting opposite a well-dressed man in a plush Central London office describing to him in detail the problems I had encountered. I was nervous, not really feeling in any way composed as I began to set out the complexities of the issues that were arising. I explained that my focus had been on securing work and doing work. The downturn was undoubtedly going to affect me, and I was looking for advice on how to reduce and restructure to react to the industry in the climate that prevailed.

The man listened with a reassuring smile and explained that this was indeed a difficult situation that lots of companies faced. His fee was a colossal amount of money. However, I had no option. I was in no position to object, and he did come to me very highly recommended. I didn't hear another thing from him for a while.

Mary and I were on holiday in Portugal when I received the phone call to tell me that the man that had been recommended was not who we thought he was. He was never going to be able to help. He had no idea how to. We had gone to the Algarve for a break, staying in a beautiful coastal villa and enjoying the fine wines and gourmet food the Algarve has to offer when the call came. This news certainly had the dampening effect of interrupting a balmy summer night, with good friends and lively music.

Things just didn't add up. I had no idea what was going or who I could trust. I remember looking across the table at one of our friends who was a barrister and considering asking for advice but in the end, I didn't.

That was the longest summer evening I have ever spent; the meal, so delicious and satisfying before the phone call; suddenly became bland and tasteless. Even the huge amount of rosé at the table had little effect. I groaned inwardly when the company we were with decided to go for a nightcap to one of the many Irish bars along the seafront, as I thought of my fate. Mary glanced sideways at me and, realising something was wrong, we made our excuses and headed back to our rented villa where I poured the whole sorry tale out over a large brandy and port.

We knew things were bad and undoubtedly going to get worse; interest rates were still sky high, the government was in trouble. When the government is in trouble, we are all in trouble I thought to myself.

That night I was so stressed. I did my best to convince Mary to leave London and bring the children back to Ireland. They could all go and live a good life there I told her, away from the mess and the worry. Just like before, Mary was going nowhere. She simply refused to go and said to me that I needed to stay and sort it out.

I didn't get a wink of sleep that night thinking about what lay ahead back in the UK. Things were bad. It was getting harder to secure good work as the economy was flatlining. I was very worried that I didn't have the right help to make sure I could save my company. I was terrified that I was going to lose everything I had built up over the years. As I tossed and turned that night, I couldn't help but think to myself, "Who the hell did I think I was to do any of that in the first place?"

That was how I came to be resting in a layby in Harrow Weald thinking about life back at home and watching one of my own machines digging across the street.

Chapter 10
Betrayals

I needed to take a step back. I decided that only thing I could do was to strip down my company and refocus. Once I had committed to the idea, I felt a great relief flooding over me. I knew exactly what I had to do, and I must admit to feeling in great form altogether as I made my plans and planned a way out of my predicament.

I was well aware of my growing reputation in the London construction world. I allowed myself to feel proud of what I had achieved just for a moment. I suppose I was always so busy chasing work that I never sat back and thought about the journey I had been on. I couldn't be bothered with that, my pleasure was the planning, of what to do next, the risk taking. It has always been more important to me to think about how I could do it rather than the looking back at what I had done.

Not bad for a lad from Kilbride, I thought to myself. I found myself grinning from ear to ear without really knowing why. I thought of a conversation earlier in the month that had opened my eyes and got me thinking. It had been explained to me that some people thought of me as somebody who was lucky. They thought I had done well but had it easy. I suppose it was because I'm not one for talking much so people imagined I achieved success without necessarily putting in the hard work.

This never bothered me before however I had taken on board some bad apples. These people I considered would be helpful to me in my business. People who would get on and do the things that had to be done. Things I had no interest in at all. It niggled me a bit when I began to hear things. Some of these people who had joined had different agendas and had underestimated me. I am an astute judge of character, but I needed a job done and, in my haste, had overlooked what my gut instinct was telling me.

What people didn't see was the risks I had to take; the house tied in against loans as collateral. My way of tackling issues without getting too excited made people think that I took it all in my stride. I was not one to chat about my problems, so people thought I had none. Unfortunately some people tried to take my business from me because they thought they could; they thought they were smarter than me, and some people wanted me out of the way. They wanted to rob me.

I knew to remain calm, and not to draw attention to myself. But I knew I had to find out what was going on. It was a hard position to be in, not knowing really who to trust. I realised that I had to put my energy into carefully listening and examining every detail of every business deal the company made. What I saw didn't please me at all and I could see that I was in a mess. Certain business dealings had been made with clauses in them that I hadn't really considered important or a threat but now realised I needed to get changed. I could see clearly what the intention had been and could also see that if I didn't do something my business would be taken from under me. These were clever people. The time had come now to stand up and get out of the situation I was in.

I ran a tight enough ship, but I had not always noticed the wolves circling. I needed advice. I needed the right advice. I didn't feel at all nervous as I explained my situation yet again; hoping that this time I was talking to somebody who had authority and the genuine expertise to help. I explained that I had received no education worth speaking about and so had welcomed people I considered to have the necessary skills into the business to help with this side of things. I was beginning to see that they were in it to see what they could make for themselves. I could see that, unless I extracted myself and off-loaded, there may not be anything left. I needed to find out how to get out of this situation. There was something in this man's response that left me feeling unsettled. My gut instinct was telling me that I was not being taken seriously. I had really laid myself bare and shared my vulnerabilities, but something didn't feel right. I felt suspicious. It had taken a lot for me to share my difficulties. Yet I was still unsure. I knew I had no choice in the matter, I knew I couldn't work again with people I didn't trust. I would just have to keep going until I found someone who felt right. It wasn't just legal stuff that concerned me; it was my pride too. I was annoyed with myself. It was with grim determination and obsession that I went ahead to continue to search for a somebody who would not only listen to me but would understand me. I knew I was coming across as naïve. I could imagine them thinking that this was a situation of my own making. I felt they were wondering how I could have let these things happen. I was among people who couldn't begin to understand my story. Why would they? It was all foreign to them and that was my problem. It was too unbelievable that I had founded a company like I had when I had no education at all behind me. These legal experts listened alright, but as much as they listened, they didn't help.

I was determined to find that one person who could work with me. One person who could delve deeper and understand; a person who could recognise that I hadn't needed education when determination was what was buried in my heart and soul. I had unwittingly tied myself in legal knots.

Each time I was told no, there was no way out. Everything was done in accordance with best practice. This made me try harder, I couldn't help myself. I kept going and my determination became an obsession; my survival instinct had overtaken, and I was determined to make myself understood.

As I told my story yet again, for what seemed like the millionth time, I got a strong feeling that the person I had just met sitting in front of me was really listening. I was a bit taken aback. This felt like somebody I could trust. I didn't encounter the glazed expressions that I had seen previously. I suppose I was more fed up than other times I recounted the tale. I was more downbeat as I spoke about my life and education.

I told my life story over again that morning, I was reliving my time in school. I could smell the turf fire burning in the damp, squalid classroom. I could see the bent heads pouring over work being copied from the teacher's squiggles on the chalk board. In my mind's eye, I was transported back and could see the distempered paint peeling off the walls to let the mushrooms sprout. I could see the wooden floorboards still wet and muddy where the wellington boots trod minutes previously. I could smell the damp. I could see the hills closing in from the high windows that let just enough light in not to have the need for a tilly lamp. Windows that were high enough not to encourage daydreaming or let restless pupils watch the pike ripple the lake surface. Most of all, I could hear the laughter as I was sent out to delve the soil and tend the garden like many before me. Big, quiet, misunderstood, underestimated.

I explained how I had cajoled Barbara into helping me to manage basic literacy just before I left for England, recognising that my little sister had managed to learn skills that I didn't have. I must have spent an hour in there talking and I wasn't interrupted once, absolutely nothing was said. I, on the other hand, had never had such a fine command of the English language as I explained how we learned to speak the English words in school. I left nothing out. I must have sounded like the Joyce country man I am, but I didn't care what anyone thought of me at all. I wasn't ashamed of anything I had or had not done, I was in fact, very proud of what I had achieved.

I couldn't stop talking that morning. I told everything, how I bought my grey tractor and how I was determined to prove I was a man of worth; how hard I worked; what drove me on; the risks I took; I even spoke about Marcus on the stack, God knows why.

Occasionally as I remembered, I was asked to slow down, they needed to make sure they understood, and I realised I had lapsed into Gaelic in my desperation to tell my story. As I finished, I looked around, noticing the ornately framed qualifications on the wall outlining a double-barrelled aristocratic sounding surname, I took in the bespoke suit and handmade shirt and thought of what Jack Chape back at home in his market stall would have made of this. The polished green leather desk was home to silver framed photographs of a smiling family holidaying on a Mediterranean yacht or frolicking around in some country pad. I sighed.

We were worlds apart. I might have made enough money to take this man and his family to the best restaurant in town but the difference between us was insurmountable. Well that's what the world in general would think. To me he was just another man making his way in life with a different set of rules, a different background. In truth I didn't care who he was as long as he took on my case and helped me regain total control of my company. I just needed somebody with his expertise to understand. After what seemed an eternity and the silence was becoming uncomfortable, he stood and offered me his hand.

Looking back now, I must have been so preoccupied. The family waited for me every evening to sit down to eat but I wasn't very good company. My health was suffering as my blood pressure increased because of the stress.

I was never so ill at ease in my life; I couldn't sleep and was self-medicating with whiskey. I felt that everything was closing in on me; everything I had worked for was at risk.

I had diversified too much, and I had left myself in a vulnerable position. Now I was paying the price, but it wasn't just me who was suffering. I had also caused stress to those around me, my family and friends. I knew I had to remain calm and focus on what was important.

That summer with its blistering hot days caused me the greatest anxiety of my life, although I was determined not to show it. As the days rolled on and the legal teams argued it out, it seemed as if there would be no end to the turmoil. I was getting so fed up with the deceit, the lies and the compromises. In truth, every time I went to a meeting my heart hammered inside my chest. I was angry but I was also quietly determined. I was being exposed and found wanting. I had begun to doubt myself, to consider myself stupid for thinking that I had any chance of making it. But I also remembered. I remembered who I was and where I came from. It was in that moment I found my inner strength.

I also felt so alone. My son Martin had come into the business but at seventeen was too inexperienced to be of any help. In any case, I couldn't do that to him. I understood and acknowledged that I could have been more diligent; I could have paid more attention to detail. But in those lofty rooms, hammering out the details of how I could get rid of the rot that seemed to have infested my company, I was weakened but not defeated.

I remember being asked about the whereabouts of somebody who had disappeared from my business.

"I don't know, I stammered, I suppose he is back at home probably in the pub having a pint, like I wish I was."

I remember them laughing; I hadn't meant to be funny at all. They were making sure that they left no stone uncovered but it was all too much for me. They obviously thought my response was hilarious.

Then, one of them reprimanded the other and instructed everyone to always remember my disability. For a split second

I was annoyed. I had never thought of myself as a disabled kind of man. I couldn't believe they considered my dyslexia a disability. I had never once in my life thought of myself like that at all and yet this is how I was being described. It was only for a split second that I was annoyed however, because I realised that it really didn't matter, I honestly didn't care what they thought of me at that stage, I just wanted them to understand the truth about me. I was a hardworking man without education but with huge ambition. That was all.

The end, when it eventually came was quite unremarkable. It had been sorted out for me. I didn't really feel anything, I was of course delighted. I was ecstatic. I couldn't help but feel that although my faith in human nature was restored, it should never have happened.

I walked to the pub that afternoon with these people who had put so much effort into helping me out. They discussed how being professional made people act in certain ways; there was a code to follow. They talked about how sometimes this could have the effect of curtailing creativity. I thought about this, and I thought about that way I think about things my freedom to be creative and not constrained. I had got myself in a bit of a situation by giving some people too free a reign, but I had freedom of thought in a way that lots of people hadn't. If the rules are understood they can be bent. I didn't know the rules and this ignorance had almost cost me my company. Rules had been used to advantage some over others and this had nearly taken me down. I didn't care for the paperwork and contracts and just went after what I wanted. That is freedom. However I just disentangled myself from a situation that should never have occurred. I remember thinking to myself that even after all I had gone through, it was a terrible state of affairs to be so constricted that you hadn't the freedom to go after what you really want.

That was a good evening as I stood up at the bar, a weight off my shoulders, chatting to those around me. I thought then how remarkable it was to be in my position. I also knew instinctively that there were others whom I had trusted that were not quite so happy with the outcome. If I was going to be successful in the future, I would have to pay more attention to the detail.

Chapter 11
Aftermath

I can honestly say that it took me a long time to recover after that. I had been successful. I had been able to get rid of those who tried to get one over on me. However, the whole experience had left me shaken. I was deeply traumatised; I couldn't believe it had happened. I had cause to stop and reflect, which is something I hadn't time to do often.

I had to admit to myself that I was driven; not driven to the point of recklessness but driven without fear of consequences. I was indeed a risk taker, and I got an adrenalin rush when focusing on my business life, but I had unwittingly left myself open to being defrauded. Although they hadn't succeeded, I paid a heavy price personally.

I felt humbled and unsure as I looked around me at my business ventures and companies. I knew that I had to make sure that never again would I be taken advantage of, but I knew that I couldn't do it all alone. I needed to ensure that I had the right people involved in my business and I knew I needed people I could trust.

While everyone was delighted with the outcome, I had a niggling doubt in my mind. I worked away as usual, but I didn't know who I could trust, and I felt so tired. Not just tired, totally exhausted. Everyone, in all of the companies started going again taking on work, but something had changed. The enjoyment simply wasn't there. I was just going through the motions. It just wasn't like me at all, and I found it difficult to concentrate, perhaps I was in shock.

Not all the companies were doing equally well, and, in my exhaustion, I became concerned about leadership level across the companies. My business model was incompatible with the direction in which some of my companies were being taken. I made the decision to offload and thankfully, this was resolved slowly but amicably. The decision was made that each company would be more successful in an individual capacity. It was inevitable that I parted ways with some, realising that sometimes it is good to cut loose and accept a partnership is over. The result was that I had slimmed down my business portfolio.

For Flannery Plant Hire the nineties were without a doubt, the worst years, what's more, as a result of losing some of the companies, I was beginning to doubt whether it was worth carrying on at all. I felt that I was adrift, and for the first time, a little unsure of my ability.

The property portfolio I had established in the early nineties was where I decided to focus all of my energy after the court case.

As a result of everything that had gone on, I decided to work alone and let the plant hire business tick along itself.

I had borrowed heavily, on the strength of my plant hire company to establish this portfolio. Once again, I put my house and business up against the loan as collateral. I purchased houses in Wembley, Cricklewood and Northolt but the houses were worth less than I paid for them.

I had to do something, so I kept renting and paying back the loans but in reality, the property business was not at all lucrative. I lost thousands of pounds. I had a property portfolio that felt like an albatross around my neck. I also had a slimmed down plant hire operation, that because of the economic downturn was enjoying questionable degrees of success.

It really wasn't a good place to be, and it took a toll on my health as I struggled to control my blood pressure. I was a broken man. When I think back now, I describe it as feeling weak; not a feeling I was accustomed to at all. Weakened, exhausted, adrift. I can safely say that I never want to experience that again and pray I never do.

At seventeen, Martin was a young man determined to become involved in the business; both Mary and I had been keen for him to stay on in school, but he was equally determined to go to work. We had lots of discussions around this; we were adamant that he should stay in school. At a parents' evening in St. Dominic's Sixth form college on Harrow on the Hill, we sat and listened to teacher after teacher tell us that Martin was clever; he had aptitude and was more eager to go to work than study. Eventually when we met his form tutor, he once again told us the same story. I thanked the teacher and that evening, Mary and I agreed that since the age of four, Martin had displayed a keenness for working with the machines and we wouldn't hold him back. We had to let Martin start to work with us to learn the business. After all, we certainly needed him. We needed people we could trust; Caroline was back working full time too and that provided great reassurance as she was so good at keeping an eye on what was going on in and around the office. It continued to be a difficult time, however, we worked steadfastly through.

My old grey tractor business model was a model I stuck to at all times, and it worked very well for me. It was simple and made economic sense, but it was not a model I shared with anyone. It was just in my head. Martin took it on board though, somehow, and he understood what others had not. As my business grew and I took more people on board, the old grey tractor model had become diluted. I didn't notice it at first, as it was simply how I operated, and I expected others to have the same values, but they didn't. Whatever the case, as I offloaded companies, I was glad to see how Martin clearly understood my "old grey tractor" way of working.

Nowadays companies would have leadership people setting out their values and vision. It would be aligned with the views of stakeholders. We just got on with it. The unintended consequences of me just getting on with it had been that some had underestimated me. I knew I had to learn from this experience. I could see that there had been a bit of general dissatisfaction among some employees. The parent company grew and others new companies were established. People had different ideas of what should be done. There was no clear leadership structure in place and while Martin knew how I operated; he was too young and too inexperienced to drive ideas forward.

Some people saw Martin coming on board as a threat and it was only down to Caroline's grit and determination to ensure that I was not being robbed of my chance to train my son in the ways of the business. Caroline was highly efficient and questioned every transaction. She made sure to keep me in the loop at all times.

Martin was gaining in knowledge and expertise. Caroline noticed that he wasn't always receiving the training we planned and agreed for him. I remember looking at this and could see what she meant. The training I had requested for Martin meant that inevitably he would hold a position of power. For some, this was a threat. My newfound wariness kicked in. I had to keep my eyes open to make sure decisions I made were being followed through.

Caroline realised that as the company was growing, more staff was needed. Occasionally, new employees tried to create factions only to come up against Caroline's wrath. She understood company values. We needed to make sure that our values were staying strong.

I began to find it increasingly difficult to trust anyone. This whole area of office politics felt like a distraction for me. It was a strange time; I just wanted to employ people to get the job done efficiently and effectively, but it seemed that no matter how much I tried to do this, things I had no interest in kept arising. It was the same thing over again.

Martin had settled in really quickly to the business. He was extremely intuitive. He really reminded me of myself as I proudly watched him navigate the business and carve out a role for himself. I felt happier to have him on board and watched his career develop with interest. Martin was doing what he was very good at doing and he was developing skills that would be of benefit to him and to the company. I was a proud father indeed.

The office politics felt never ending, once one problem was cleared up another one arrived. What I noticed was that in every case, it involved somebody who had different ideas to mine about how my company should be run. I decided to add once again to our portfolio. Even though this new business was in a totally new direction, we were excited to give it a go. It wasn't until we sat down to evaluate the financial success that things turned a little sour. I drafted Caroline in and poured over the books; it didn't take long for discrepancies to arise. This was a devastating blow for us. Once again, greed, jealousy and a lack of integrity had created problems. It was a very hard lesson. It was difficult for us to believe; it was so incomprehensible that we genuinely thought there must be mitigating circumstances. We searched. We could find none; the venture had soured for us, and the business was eventually sold on. This seemed incredible to me, as once again somebody who I trusted had let me down.

I worried about the effect of this on my family. They had some knowledge of what was happening; I couldn't keep everything from them. They had a knowledge about human behaviour that I certainly never did when I left Kilbride and it worried me. Around this time, my second son, Patrick, came to work in the company. Together, Martin and Patrick made a great team. I was delighted to see them work together but my niggling worries continued. I thought constantly about everything I had been through, how dealing with petty jealousies and greed impacted on my family. I think that angered me more than losing money. I could see how their experiences of watching me meant they started out their working lives with totally different perspectives. I thought about the lessons I had learned from my own upbringing and could see that I never had to experience anything like what they had. Nobody had ever deliberately tried to do a bad turn in my family circle, nobody had ever tried to keep me down. We had been brought up to share what we had, to help when we could and to work hard for our money. It angered me that my sons had been exposed to the opposite of this at a young age and I was desperately afraid that this would blight their future determination. I didn't want them to become people who found it difficult to trust others.

I am keen to make sure my family realise that even when people let us down; even when people we trusted show that they are not worthy of that trust, we must behave in a dignified way and not let the issues of others cloud how we respond. Nobody goes through life without getting hurt but it is how we respond that makes us the people we are. I do not look back and wonder why people behave in certain ways; I have no time for that; I simply move on. I bear no grudges, as I have too much to do. That's why I am not going into detail about these events. It doesn't do anyone any good. Take the learning from it and move on. That's my attitude.

Betrayal is a terrible thing. I understand human nature and recognise the need that exists in people to better themselves. I fully understand that there are times when this need drives people to behave in ways that they know to be wrong. I understand temptation, I understand greed and have seen how power can corrupt. I can see how the need to control can lead people to exert influences on situations to the detriment of others. I can even see the blinkered reality of those who have underestimated me.

I also know that I will never let any of the above define me as an individual. I know that to dwell on this would make me a bitter and resentful person. I refuse to give anyone the power to do that. I know I think positively; I look at what I have achieved and am thankful. When I am asked about my feelings about people who have wronged me, I can honestly say I never, ever dwell on it. They did what they did, and they must live with it.

Chapter 12
Tractors, Celebrations and Honda 50s

In 2000 we decided that we would move out from the suburbs and out into the countryside. I really wanted to have more land to perhaps do a little bit of farming or to have the option to keep animals in the future. Our friend Ian continued to tell us all about how wonderful life was living further out from London. He had been keen for us to do this earlier when he moved to Buckinghamshire himself. He was well settled and pleased with what that county had to offer in terms of services and education. We were ready for a change but once again we were worried; we would miss our lovely neighbours.

Arthur was a lovely old gentleman who lived across the road with his wife Alice. He really was the quintessential English gentleman with his impeccable manners and gentle nature. Arthur was retired and his family had all flown the nest so by a strange set of circumstances, he became a childminder for our son Paul. Arthur used to come to the house each day to collect Paul and bring him to Montessori, and while he was waiting, used to tend to our houseplants. Paul loved Arthur and Arthur made sure Paul was polite and had lovely manners. It was a lovely arrangement that suited all of us as and led to us becoming firm friends.

We had great neighbours who looked out for each other and helped one another out. John and Bridie O'Brien had also moved from Holland Road to Sudbury, and we were always in touch with them.

In our search for more space, we found a house called 'The Old Workhouse' and it was as if it was meant to be, because it was situated just beside the site I had worked on when I got my first machine.

On first sight it was a ramshackle building, but it was easy to see the possibilities. I felt that I had stepped back into rural Ireland when I saw that house and the surrounding land; this was ideal. 'The Old Workhouse' had been a refuge for the poor of the parish of Ruislip and the irony of that was not lost on me as we set about the restoration. The grounds held most interest for me; we had ample room for growing vegetables, and I decided I would set up a field to have rescue donkeys and maybe keep an old grey tractor. I thought I might even buy myself a Honda 50!

Mary restored the old Aga and installed a half door in the kitchen with a view out on to the field; it felt like a little piece of Ireland in Ruislip. Mary has a talent for making our home cosy; she put an Irish dresser against the wall, and pride of place in the kitchen was the table covered in a blue oil cloth. It was just like home.

Shortly after moving in, I travelled to a tractor auction. The auction was filled with tractors of every shape and form. On show were top of the range tractors with the best of equipment installed, but they held no interest for me. That was not what I was after; and then I saw it. Not as shiny, not as big, not as well designed as the others and consigned to a corner. Hidden and forlorn. I knew the minute I saw it that I had to have it; an old grey tractor. I was a happy man the day I made my maiden journey driving into Ruislip. I still make that journey as often as I can and enjoy the looks the tractor gets from passers-by and chatting with people as I stop along the road.

When I moved into the Old Workhouse and bought the grey tractor, I also bought a Honda 50. I hadn't been able to take either prized possession over from Kilbride, so I thought to myself that this was an acceptable indulgence. I had great fun riding the Honda 50 around the house and up through the fields, imagining myself back in Kilbride, cycling around the lake without a care in the world.

I have a lot to be thankful for and, without going into detail, I I like to show my gratitude by involving myself in charity work. My friend Ian was involved in a particular charity and asked me to clear a driveway at its head office in Buckinghamshire. It transpired that the charity had the use of a very grand house, but the driveway had seen better days and was becoming a problem. The charity couldn't afford to do the work and as Ian knew we had a few machines, he asked us to get involved. I had other ideas however! I decided I wanted to do it myself! I remember being quite excited that morning as I pulled up to patch up the driveway; I was out on the road again and delighted with myself. I must admit to getting a kick out of the whole situation as the trustees came over and asked me to make sure I thanked the owner for his help; they had no idea of the identity of their machine driver for the day. I don't mind saying that I made a terrific job of that drive; I worked until not only every pothole was infilled, but the whole drive was cleared and flattened.

A few weeks later, Mary and I received a gilt-edged invitation from the lord and lady of the manor to go along for afternoon tea as a thank you for our work to help them fix the driveway. We had a tour of the grand house and gardens and were treated to a splendid afternoon tea. They were both so lovely and really appreciative of the hard work of our driver that day, who they commended highly for going above and beyond any expectations. I never made them any the wiser.

I ngan fhios don Saol is fearr a bheadh ann. (unknown to the World it is better to be)

I am thankful for this attitude and work ethic instilled in me from my family. Mary and I brought our children up to work hard, value money and keep their counsel. When our children were old enough, they worked for their pocket money. We made sure we never lived in a frivolous manner; we tried to be generous but were sensible with money and kept a tight rein on spending. Apart from the odd occasion as a treat, we shopped in cheaper supermarkets and never lived beyond our means. This is important to both of us, as it is who we are.

I'm delighted to say that we have kept in touch with most of our old neighbours, as well as lots of people from home. We have had great parties in the Workhouse going on until every tune has been played and every last song sung.

Chapter 13
Family Man

I am not a man given to having big displays of wealth; I don't need feel the need to travel the world, live in luxury hotels and drive fine cars. I am much happier driving my old grey tractor and tinkering under the bonnet. I suppose that is why I'm so happy living at the Old Workhouse as I have plenty of room to indulge myself in the things I want to enjoy.

That's not to say that my family have not tried to influence me in this way. I ordered a Bentley, and it really is magnificent, I am delighted with it, but without the family urging me on I would never have ordered it. I'll never forget the looks I got the first time I took it out. I was driving along minding my own business when I suddenly became aware of people staring. I was a little worried at first, and then I reminded myself of what I was driving. It is the height of luxury and lovely to drive but I had to be prepared to be stared at. With some friends, I took it for a run up the A40 to celebrate the new car and get used to the stares. We had a great time enjoying the car, and it does feel amazing to drive. As good, as this felt, I felt just as proud as I did when I took friends around the lake on the Honda 50.

I have also been booked to go on an exotic holiday by my wife and family. They decided I would enjoy a holiday to St Lucia, to a health spa. I hate long haul flights, mostly because of my size.

I get so uncomfortable in planes, however I reluctantly agreed to go. I don't mean to sound ungrateful, but the fact is that it's really not my thing at all. I was booked into first class, so I had extra leg room while Mary and Julie sat in business class because we didn't want to waste money. I remember feeling so uncomfortable in first class. I didn't enjoy it one bit, I couldn't relax at all and spent my time up at the bar. During the flight, Mary came to find me to see how I was enjoying first class travel, expecting to see me lying back in the bed sipping champagne but there I was, standing at the bar chatting to the attendant with a bottle of beer. I think Mary wished that she had put me in business class and enjoyed first class herself. I did enjoy some treatments when I was in St. Lucia, with a pedicure every day, but the reality was I was only doing it to pass the time. The truth is that I would rather have been back home working with my tractor.

I recognise that I tend to have an obsessive personality, and that personality has for the most part been focused on work, so I began to try to focus on other things apart from work. I bought a few donkeys to keep in the upper field, and I enjoyed looking after them, stubborn, unforgiving characters that they are. Fr Tim and I used to work together, fixing fences, and mending gates. Tim had some beehives in the upper field and provided us with lots of honey. We used to joke that although both of us had been living in England for so long, we never did get rid of the longing to be working on the farm.

By the time we moved to Ruislip, Martin and Patrick had already moved out. I suppose ours was a traditional family and we expected that of the boys, to go out into the world as soon as they could. Maria, Paul and Julie moved to Ruislip with us. Eventually of course, the older children met their partners, got married, bought family homes and settled.

It is a true blessing my family are all happy and settled. I enjoy the grandchildren who are regular visitors to our home. For me, the perfect Sunday evening is one where family call round, friends visit and I light up the barbecue, crack open a few bottles of wine, and bring out the accordion to start a sing song just as we used to do back home. Just like home, I love to see generations together, to hear about how everyone is doing, how work is going and share any news from home. I am at my happiest then. Mary is such a good host, and there is always plenty to eat and drink. We miss her brother Jimmy who has passed away. In his later years, he lived in his own place on the grounds of the workhouse after a life of travelling. Jimmy, an accomplished musician, often had his friends over to play for us. He would arrive up at the house with his steak in one hand and his carry out in the other, always with a cigarette hanging from his mouth. He loved the company; and the children adored him as they spent the long evenings listening to him play.

I am proud to say that Mary and I kept up our friendships based across the wide spectrum of people we met. Mary and I are so grateful for the opportunities we were given in England; we are very proud of our adopted country. Mary loves the royal family. We have certainly had a good living in England, which we would never have been able to do if we stayed at home. England has been good to us and we don't like to hear people knock it. We have all had opportunities to come over and work hard. I am very happy living in England, even though to all intents and purposes our home is as Irish as it can be outside the country itself. But we have made lots of English friends. I appreciate the English culture and respect the traditions and heritage of this great nation.

The multicultural society that is England today is happily reflected in our circle of friends. We are grateful to them for sharing and celebrating their different cultures. One of Mary's favourite things to do is to get everyone around our long dining room table for a homecooked meal. Mary sets the table as her mother did, with two big bowls of spuds at each end and two sets of everything to make sure people can reach for the food and that there is plenty of it. So important is it to Mary that there are enough spuds for everyone that before Patrick's wedding to Laura in the beautiful Castle Coombe, she pre-arranged a visit with the chef to make sure he understood that alongside the fine cuisine planned for the wedding breakfast, each table had to have at least two bowls of spuds. Mary had a horror of anyone being hungry for a few spuds as they enjoyed their exquisite meal. The chef wasn't too pleased, but he knew who was boss!

There is one place I am always happy to travel to outside of Ireland and that is to our villa in Portugal. When Maria saw it for the first time, I remember her asking me if it was true, that we were rich.

"Girleen" I asked, "Why would you ask such a thing?"

She went on to tell me that that at school, in year five, a boy in her class had told her she was rich because he had heard his parents talking about our yard in Wembley. She said she didn't believe him. She went on to say that in year seven, she had arrived in school on own clothes day in new Levi jeans, Levi shirt and Reebok trainers only to suffer embarrassment when some other children looked at her in envy, stating that she was indeed a rich kid. I had no idea what she was talking about, but she explained that she was severely embarrassed by this and totally confused. She heard us worry about money. Maria was in full flow at this stage, the normally reserved and quiet child, that she was, now looking accusingly at me and stated that I had told her that I was a hairdresser. She believed it until her cousin Orla back home in Kilbride had told her the truth. Maria was becoming more agitated as I bent up laughing; she didn't think it was funny at all, shouting at me that in Kilbride she was seen as the spoilt English girl. Orla was so much more streetwise, blagging lifts to Ballinrobe to the dances that they couldn't even get into. They just wanted to go to Supermac's and have the craic on the way home. What is the truth she wanted to know, looking incredulously around the villa, "Are we rich or what?" But in the same breath wanting to know if she could take her friends over for a holiday. I looked at my beautiful daughter; no wonder she is confused, I thought to myself. Night after night she heard us worrying about who wasn't paying up; the troubles we had getting drivers. We never sat and congratulated ourselves on how well we were doing, ever. We were always striving, Mary and I, always looking for the next opportunity and that is all Maria knew. I smiled down at her tear-stained face and said, "Of course you can bring your friends over here to visit".

We raced down to the beach that evening, myself, Mary, Paul, Julie, Maria and I got to work on the most wonderful sand crocodile to cheer them up. I was delighted with the results and even more so when passers-by started throwing in a couple of escudo.

There have been a few times when I have thought about how things have turned out. There is no doubt that wealth brings great security, great comfort and a great sense of fulfilment. Even for somebody like me who doesn't feel quite at ease with the trappings of wealth, I can of course see that having a lovely house, a villa in Portugal, eating out whenever the notion takes us and buying clothes when I need to or indulging in hobbies such as driving an old grey tractor, is a comfort and blessing not shared by all. I do worry for my family, what father doesn't? And I also wonder what legacy I have left.

I thought about this one evening as I walked up to the back field, the hedgerows secluding my little bit of Ireland in Ruislip. I passed the happy looking donkeys who had gathered in the hope of a few nuts and heard, rather than saw, Fr Tim's beehives as I plodded on, lost in my thoughts. I wanted to leave a legacy to my family.

We had done, as our families before us had done; the boys were encouraged to go out to work at the business; indeed there was an expectation that they did this. It wasn't as if we had actively encouraged it; they could have done whatever took their fancy, but they haven't done that. Paul is now doing well in the company working alongside his brothers and taking over some roles to release the older sons to grow our family business.

What about the girls? I have two bright, articulate young women and I am immensely proud of them.

I walked on, considering how the choices I made have affected my family in ways I could never have imagined. Maria had trained to become a teacher, and she enjoyed this but and when the opportunity came to buy an after-school company, we supported her decision. She changed direction and is now successfully building up a fine business. Julie, the youngest, has recently begun to work as an accountant in the business.

I was confident that my children were equipped to do whatever it was they wanted to; they could handle life situations brought on by being in my family very well. I hadn't brought them up to see themselves as rich kids and didn't want others to see them like that either.

The villa in Portugal was intended to be used during every long school holiday. It was situated in a quiet town where the children would be able to roam the streets freely as teenagers and it had a golf course nearby for Mary. I used to love taking off on the many cycle routes around Alvor. It was an exciting time seeing the building plans and designing a place where we could bring family and friends. Happily, lots of our family do come to stay and our friends visit frequently too. We have many happy memories of nights in the mountains feasting on lamb for Julie's birthday in February, as well as days out at the waterparks and on the sea. We made lots of friends in Alvor but somehow it never took over from Ireland as our main holiday destination. Lots of the friends we made visited us in Ireland during the summer.

This was because as lovely as Alvor was, Ireland was where we had our main family holidays. We would go back as much as we could when the grandparents were alive. My sister Nora and her girls lived next door and were like a second family to us. The children would run into "Granny's" the minute we would get home and receive an open-armed welcome and a table full of food after our long journey. "Honestly, you think nobody was fed at all in England" I would joke. My mother, who would never have set foot in a pub in her younger years, used to delight at the prospect of accompanying myself and Mary to 'The Larches' or over to 'Maire Luke's' where she would have a Bailey's. I was so happy to see her enjoying herself like that. In Ireland, I could see the children blossom as they roamed wild; Maria, with her cousin Orla, enjoyed playing pool and managing to get Mintos, Cadbury's chocolate, crisps and coke for every round the adults had in the pub. Summer days were filled with fishing trips, picnics and running free. When we were out on the lake, I used to point to the old schoolhouse by the road, now derelict, and say that was where I had my primary school, my secondary school and my university. The children would gaze at it, wide eyed and innocent. Julie could never understand how that small place was a university too!

When Petersburg Outdoor Pursuits Centre opened in 1988, the children had even more to do back in Ireland. They loved it. Petersburg House was the ancestral home of a branch of the Lynch family of Galway. The family were granted land around the shores of Lough Mask under a policy of 'Surrender and Re-grant' [3] and the 'Big House' was built in 1715. The children were confused by the name, and I explained that there was no Russian connection! Peter Lynch just wanted the place to be

---

[3] Policy introduced by Henry VII of England. If a Gaelic lord surrendered his lands to the crown and swore loyalty, he could stay on the land which in turn could be inherited by his sons.

called after himself. I was happy in the knowledge that the children had plenty to occupy them; I wanted them to really appreciate an Irish childhood, make friends and live simply.

Around this time, an incident that had occurred back in Sudbury, with Julie when we had decorators in the house. Unknown to either Mary or I, Julie had been carefully observing every move the painter was making. When he was lifting the carpet to paint the skirting boards, she very helpfully pointed out to him that if he just lifted the floorboards in that area, he would see some money daddy had hidden there. Luckily for us, the painter was an honest man and told us straight away. But the incident brought home to me the fact that when they were off school, I would rather have my children running wild back home in Kilbride without a care in the world rather than sitting in London telling anybody who would listen where I had my money stashed!

We laughed about it afterwards, but I didn't want my children to be concerned about money. I wanted them to appreciate the wild beauty of Mayo and Galway, to learn songs from the hearth and listen to stories handed down from generation to generation. I wanted them to have a sense of belonging, to truly understand where they came from and who they were. That is why we ended up going to Kilbride every long summer holiday and why Portugal, no matter how beautiful it was, never really took over from Kilbride in our minds as a summer holiday destination.

My daughters make me proud every day. Julie, who used to like nothing more than going out fishing with our neighbours and cousins, racing onto the islands, with a picnic in hand developed a wander lust. This cheeky little girl, who was so impatient and would refuse to sit down quietly in the boat and wait for the fish to bite, made us so proud when she qualified as an accountant. She worked for a while and then took herself off, using her savings wisely, to travel with friends to Australia and the Far East, sometimes travelling alone. Julie being the youngest, had a different upbringing than the others. She was taught all manner of rude behaviour by her older siblings, and this caused her to get into trouble at school. Poor Julie spent many hours in the head teacher's room but had an answer for everything. Despite this, she matured into a lovely young woman. As well as having a host of naughty older siblings to contend with, Julie had more time with myself and Mary as a child. Our business was established, we were around more and could spend time with her. I used to love getting up and making her a bacon croissant every morning before I would drive her to school. It reminded me of my own father making the breakfast for us when he returned home.

Our Parish Priest Fr Tim and I used to mend fences and look after the land around the house, just as we would have done back home. Like me, he was a farmer at heart and had been a firm family friend since our Sudbury days and often came to visit after Mass on Sundays. We gave him a spot to put up beehives and he was delighted to provide us with honey. Fr Tim came to

Ireland to visit us too. He used to come with us when we went out fishing and picnicking on the many islands in the lake and even said Mass on one of them one summer. In truth, these things were more important to me than any fancy car. Despite the fact that I had a lovely house, a fine life and money in my pocket, I liked to be reminded of simpler times.

Chapter 14
Legacy

When I was first asked to share my story, I hadn't a clue what I was going to talk about. I have lived in this world for a long time, over seven decades and have lots of different experiences. I have met many good people and some people I would rather forget. I have laughed with family and friends and shed tears as good people passed away. What's it all about? I hear people ask that question a lot. I hear people joke about pockets on a shroud or tow bars on a hearse. How would I like to be remembered? Is it as Paddy Flannery who founded Flannery Plant Hire, well yes of course. But it has become clearer to me as I spend time thinking over past events, that what is important to me, is that my children and grandchildren really know who I am. Then, by knowing me and knowing Mary as young people, with hopes and dreams the same as anyone else, that might help them understand where they came from, understand our legacy and most importantly understand exactly who they are too.

The grandchildren are small now and know me as the grandfather who sings, "The Muffin Man"; the eejit who pretends to be a hairdresser one day and a doctor the next; somebody who talks nonsense to them to make them laugh.

Nobody wants to think about when they are gone but it comes to us all, and I want my family to know my story.

I want them to realise that I was a man who would never accept that I couldn't achieve what I wanted to achieve. When I came up against a situation where it looked bad for me, I found another way to do things. I am a stubborn man for sure; I am quiet. I am a deep thinker, and I don't waste words. I know what I want, and I go for it.

I want my grandchildren to know all this about me, and I also want them to realise that I have always tried to be straight with people, to respect every man for who he is and most importantly to walk away from those who have harmed me. I am not one to dwell on what I can't change. I have met those along the way who have wished me harm. It is impossible to build up a business like ours without having some run ins with people. I suppose I would like to say that although I might never have said much, I always realised when people were trying to get one over on me. If I never said anything it was because I had my reasons and not because I didn't realise or see-through people. I just didn't think the people who wished me harm were worth sweating about. I am good at parking things like that and moving on.

Probably because I am driven and have always been, I don't see much point in wondering why certain people acted as they did.

Since I was a schoolboy back in Kilbride, I realised education was never going to help me, and that I had to find another way to follow my ambition. That other way was hard work, but something I have never been afraid of is hard work. It is the making of a person to receive a day's wages for a good day's work. What is done with the wages has always been equally important to me. I have cut corners in my life to save money. I have lived in poor accommodation and scrimped on food. I have rationed my pints at the weekend, all so I could save as much as I could.

This habit has been a hard habit to break. I know that sometimes some of my family wish I would spend more on myself, but I really don't need to. I do of course love it when they spend money on lovely places to stay and invite myself and Mary. They never tell me how much these places cost and even if they ever do tell me, I know they don't tell me the right price. They spare me that much! I can't help it; I am who I am.

I can see now that my drive, ambition and refusal to accept defeat has been a constant in my life. I don't really know where I got this drive from; I suppose it could have been as a result of my upbringing, of seeing my parents strive and succeed. I always knew that wherever I was, I had to succeed. I was hungry for success, but I have never had a plan. I just looked at every opportunity that came my way and thought about how I could benefit from it. If I could see a way of using an opportunity, I threw myself into it. If not, I simply walked away.

In my earlier years, work was all I thought about. I had a deep desire to be the best at what I did, and this spurred me on. I never stopped working, I never took the money I made and spent it; I ploughed it all back into my business so that it would become even better than before.

Nowadays, cycling has become my new obsession. I cycle about forty to fifty miles every day and I get great pleasure from that. I love being out in nature and during the recent pandemic, it was a godsend to be out on the road.

I have built a fine legacy for my family to enjoy, and my heart's desire is that they are proud of their heritage. I want them to know that they too must put in the effort to be the best that they can be.

I want my grandchildren to remember me as a simple man. I was never educated but have always believed in myself. I have always tried to do right by people. I don't want to boast but I have always known I would make something of myself in England.

In more recent years there is more emphasis placed on academic qualifications and because of this not many wanted to work in the plant hire industry. I also knew that this wasn't right. I certainly know that not everybody is cut out to go to university. But I know this isn't right. Not everybody is cut out for university. I know that my tractor driving days back in Kilbride gave me a great advantage. This experience helped me learn to drive. But I wondered how young fellas today who wanted to be machine drivers or fitters would learn. In 2021 Flannery's were approached by Balfour Beatty. They wanted to partner with us to build a skills hub to train the drivers of the future. So, Flannery Balfour Beatty Operator Skills hub was born. This is a venture of which I am really proud. I see myself in each of those young people who sign up for training. The facility uses state of the art simulators as well as the latest semi-automated vehicles to prepare plant operators and apprentices for the modern-day digitally enabled construction site. I'm delighted with this; I like to see young people getting trained and I know I'm not alone in this. In 2022 Gavin Williamson the then education secretary visited our provision and because of this we gained nationwide media coverage. Imagine me being on prime-time television because of my involvement in a training facility to educate young people for careers in construction. I can scarcely believe it.

The industry has changed massively since I started Flannery Plan Hire Oval. Ltd and all for the better. We are still a family run company; we have built up a great team around us who share our collective family vision.

Some of my good friends have since passed on and I miss them. As I get older, I can't help but think about things a little more, wondering what life is all about. Never in my wildest dreams would I have imagined the life I live now. But then again, I was always focused on any opportunity that came my way and didn't imagine a poor life for myself either.

I am blessed to be close to my family. They are all successful in their chosen paths and all like to come around at weekends when our house is full of the noise and laughter of grandchildren, just like Kilbride used to be years ago. The family bring friends round often for food, drinks and usually a sing song until the small hours. And it's there you will find me, sitting in the corner, pint in hand, waiting for the chance to take out my accordion, that is what makes me happy.

Rothaí Mór an tsaoil. (the circle of life) old Irish proverb

Recently, I have been thinking about how to finish off this memoir. I feel healthy and happy, full of life and not in the least ready to finish anything off. I couldn't quite think of an ending for a life that is still in full swing. Then something happened that really made me think and take stock. I was invited with Mary to take become freemen of the city of London. All I knew about this was that when you have freedom of the city, you are permitted to drive a flock of sheep across London Bridge. A strange thing to do for sure but I was up for it! I did a bit of research and found out that to be a freeman in years gone by meant that you are not the property of a Lord and that you can earn money and own land. It meant you were free to trade and that you had to belong to a livery company who would make sure that your produce would come up to standard. Livery companies were formed by bakers, carpenters, goldsmiths, plumbers and they made sure that they looked after each other. They trained apprentices and then after they had spent their time training, they became yeomen and then freemen. I liked the sound of that, as it's a bit like the work we were doing to make sure young people learned their trade. The livery companies all had the same outlook; to educate the young, to care for the elderly and to support those in need, while all the time making sure their product or service was of top quality. This has been going on since medieval times and was something that everyone can still understand today. Mary and I were delighted to take part. We found out that we were nominated because of our charity work as well as how we operate as a company that benefits the city of London, so it was a big privilege. We went off with family and friends to the guildhall. It was all pomp and ceremony and the people there couldn't have been nicer. They were all dressed up in their finery but took the time to really explain to all of us what the ceremony was all about and even took us on a tour of the building to hear about other people who had got the freedom. We got our photo taken with a model sheep to remind us that we could now drive over London Bridge with our flock. In the olden days this was a great privilege because freemen didn't have to pay a toll on the bridge when they took their flock to market. Also, we found out about another privilege, that being a freeman meant we could ask any policeman to take us home after a night in the pub. I was told that there was no point in trying this one out nowadays! As we progressed through the ceremony, I was taken aback to realise that when mine and Mary's name was inserted into the ledger, they also inserted our parents' names. Imagine that both sets of parents' names recorded forever in the City of London, along with the likes of Florence Nightingale and Winston Churchill. It really made me smile when I realised that our parents, who had life hard, who worked tirelessly to help us get along, were now recorded in the Guild Hall in London. These people who were from the land, who knew every crag and rock along Lough Mask, whose mother tongue was Irish and who lived life alongside the rhythm of the seasons, were recognised in this way as contributing to life in the City of London. Now that was what made everything worthwhile.

Life has a strange way of including the most unexpected events. There's plenty for me to do; I have the energy and thank God I have my health so I will pack my lunch, fill my flask and head off on my bike. I will stop for a while at a spot where I can pull up and eat my sandwiches, drink my tea and think sure, why wouldn't I do this, don't I deserve it?

WHY WOULDN'T I?

Acknowledgements

To all who contributed to this story, I am deeply indebted. I have used bits of stories and intertwined them in various places, sometimes with names changed. The essence of all of the many stories I heard during the course of research into this book is included. I have taken some liberties with events and actions for the purposes of engaging the reader. Some stories are not told in depth and characters have been alluded to but not named.

To those who gave freely of their time, Francis and Fr Tim who are sadly no longer with us, may they rest in peace.

To Katie Boyle and Aoife Boyle for their hard work proof reading and editing this book.

To Sean Donnelly for his patience and advice on design, printing and publishing.

I spent many lovely evenings in the company of Paddy and Mary and have tried to weave their stories together using Paddy's voice. This is a story of courage and of wisdom, of strength and determination.

This is Paddy's story.

Printed in Dunstable, United Kingdom